The Future of Investing is Here

Welcome Aboard.

We ride at dawn.

What I've learned in my 45 years of being in the markets

Wilfred P. Brockmann MBA (Fin), FCSI

Illustrations by Wilfred Brockmann

Published by Wilfred Brockmann

For information, contact wilf@brockmann.com

The Future of Investing is Here

Welcome Aboard.

We ride at dawn.

Written by Wilfred Brockmann

To:

Everyone who has that yearning and curiosity to learn and grow more for the betterment of themselves and others.

Wilf

Table of Contents

Welcome

I want to first congratulate you on being here and showing your unwavering determination to get ahead and strive for more. Because you deserve to have better. My name is Wilf Brockmann, and I'll be your guide, mentor, and coach. Picking up this book tells me you are serious about making money in the markets.

Maybe you are tired of listening to that annoying guy down the hall and the tips he says he is getting. Or your brother-in-law with all of his successful Bitcoin ventures? You want to do better and feel more in control. Perhaps you have this feeling, this urge that you can do better. You may have many reasons to be dissatisfied with your Financial Advisor. Maybe you're perplexed by their inability to outperform the index. You've grown tired of fancy words or phrases masking underperformance. You're ready for a change, and that's commendable.

There is nothing wrong with wanting more. You are not alone; I am with you each step of the way, dedicated to your success. It takes a confident individual to take responsibility for their future. Take a deep breath; you are about to seize control of your destiny. Yes, I know it can be nerve-racking at first, but no one will be more dedicated and have your future in their heart than YOU.

Many people view investing and trading as a hobby, something to dabble in, and if that is you, then great. Thank you for coming along. If you view this as a personal business, I want to ask: Would your boss hire you or fire you right now? I am here to help you get that promotion to CEO of your investing life.

Over the last four decades, I have dedicated my life to being a financial advisor, coach, and friend to countless clients and colleagues. Through my experiences and dedication, I have gained valuable knowledge and insights about investing and the markets. I have dedicated this book to sharing many of the critically important aspects I have learned. The financial world can be complex and challenging to navigate, but with dedication and hard work, one can gain a deep understanding of how the markets work. Like in life, investing teaches us valuable lessons that we can only learn through perseverance, determination, and active participation. I have worked tirelessly in a profession that I love, and my passion for helping others achieve financial success has only grown stronger over the years. I am not saying it will be easy on this adventure you and I are embarking on - but I will be at your side.

I believe anyone can become a successful investor and trader if they are willing to put in the effort and learn from their experiences. I will share my insights and teachings in this book to help you navigate the markets and make informed investment decisions. From understanding risk management to recognizing market trends to dealing with one's emotions, a wealth of knowledge is waiting to be unlocked. I have had more than my share of ups and disappointments. I have sometimes laid on the mat too long, wallowing in self-pity. But let's be honest with each other. Nobody cares about you until you win. So let's win. Let's win together.

As a financial advisor, I have witnessed both success stories and setbacks, but one thing remains constant—the importance of continuous learning. I have dedicated myself to staying up-to-date on market trends and investment strategies, and I encourage you to do the same. By arming yourself with the knowledge and expertise found within this book, you can skillfully navigate the financial landscape and make sound investment choices.

There is always more to learn as you constantly strengthen and grow in your understanding of the markets. Investing is a journey that requires patience, discipline, and a willingness to adapt to changing circumstances. It is a process and not a destination. I hope to impart the wisdom and insights I have gained to help you on your own investing journey. I am confident that anyone can become a successful investor with dedication and perseverance. By learning from my experiences and insights shared in this book, you can take control of your financial future and achieve your investment goals. Anything is possible with the right knowledge and mindset. Thank you for allowing me to be a part of your journey, and I wish you success and prosperity in your investing endeavors.

Having the best tools and state-of-the-art systems is only part of the equation; emotional control is the other. This Book is not just a guide; it's a companion on your personal journey. Like most traders and investors, you're not alone in the mental game you're engaged in. It's a battle fought in that space between your left and right brains, pitting you, the confident trader, against the doubtful, timid self. This book is here to help you understand and master this psychological battle.

The success of your trades often depends on your ability to overcome self-doubt, fear, and anxiety. Therefore, I have written this book about you and our journey together. It is an essential read for anyone looking to improve their trading performance in this fast-paced, high-pressure environment, which constantly challenges traders and investors.

This book will explore the psychological aspects of trading, exploring how our emotions, biases, and experiences influence our decision-making process. By understanding the mental game of trading, you can learn to identify and overcome the psychological barriers that hold you back from achieving your full potential as a trader. One of the key messages of this book is that trading is not just about analyzing charts and following trends. It's about mastering your mind and emotions, staying disciplined in the face of uncertainty, and cultivating a mindset of confidence and resilience.

By developing a strong mental game and using the right tools, you can consistently make profitable trades and outperform the competition. Through real-life examples, practical exercises, and expert advice, "*The Future of Investing is Here*" guides you on a journey of self-discovery and personal growth. It teaches you how to cultivate a positive mindset, manage your emotions effectively, and develop the mental toughness needed to succeed.

So, if you're tired of feeling stuck in a cycle of self-doubt and underperformance, it's time to take control of your mental game and become the confident, successful trader you will be. "*The Future of Investing is Here*" is your roadmap to mastering your mind and the markets. Thank you for grabbing your copy today as we start our journey towards trading success together.

Having the right mindset is only part of the equation. The other part is having a tool kit full of proven techniques, strategies, and methods that are adaptive to market changes.

By experimenting with and then discarding things that don't work, one figures out the true lessons of investing and the markets. During this painstaking learning process, it occurred to me that maybe someone else who is a wealth seeker would like to learn some of these lessons. For that, I am grateful for your attendance and joining me.

Throughout this book, you will hear of my core beliefs and foundational principles, and you can treat them knowing they are my biases, but you will always know where I am coming from. I have a quote taped on one of my monitors that I look at daily. It is from an unlikely individual, but I feel her quote is very relevant to the journey we are about to embark on.

"Yesterday is gone. Tomorrow has not yet come. We have only today. Let us begin."

- St. Mother Teresa of Calcutta.

But first, a couple of housekeeping matters.

- Relax. Try reading this book straight through once for enjoyment. It's not a competition, and there are no exams. Take it easy and have some fun with it.

- I've asked you to read this book critically but try not to argue with me on the first run-through. If you have a question, take note and continue. You may find the answer further on. Even as you come up against points you have trouble accepting (and you will), don't get hung up on them immediately. Read the book to grasp the fundamental logic, then go back if needed, and work on the things that trouble you.

- This book does not claim to identify the next NVDA or the next best thing since sliced bread, but it will tell you how to stay with them and get out of them when they perform poorly. You will not get rich overnight, but will get rich over time.

- When presenting any book to a general audience on a semi-technical topic like investing, we will encounter some who find it too complicated and some who find it too elementary. To the 'too complicated' group, I will try not to use jargon and will explain it when I do. To the 'too basic' group, think about how you could expand on what I am said for your own benefit.

- I will interchange the words investor and trader throughout the book, seeing them as the same. We are both at different times. I see a trader as one who is considering, debating, entering trades, reviewing, and implementing the tactic component of the plan in the now and in the current time frame. An investor is one who is considering a long-term perspective and views the plan from a strategic point of view. Sometimes we wear one hat and sometimes both hats.

- I will encourage you to smile as much as possible as you read the book and go about your daily life. The act of smiling triggers the release of endorphins. These chemicals boost your mood, decrease stress, and foster a sense of tranquility. Smiling also improves your perceived approachability, which can heighten your opportunity for social support when faced with challenging circumstances. Once, while smiling and pondering several things in an elevator, someone asked me if I was on drugs. I replied yes and got off on my floor.

What this book will do for you and want it won't

Through this book, I will endeavor to help create your financial freedom. Financial freedom is a goal that many people strive for, but few can achieve. Picking up this book tells me you want freedom as much as I do. Freedom is the ability to live without worrying about the financial instability that surrounds us, where money is no longer a limiting factor. Wealth is indeed freedom. It is not about a specific number in your bank account or the accumulation of material possessions, but the sense of security and peace of mind that comes with knowing you have the resources to live your desired life because you deserve it. Let me say that again: you deserve it.

Plenty of families with modest net worth feel wealthy beyond measure because they have financial security and stability. Additionally, wealthy families with millions of dollars constantly fear losing their fortune and never experience true wealth as they crave more.

Wealth is about the freedom to make choices without constraints. It allows you to pursue your passions and live the life you dream of. It will allow you to work because you love what you do, not because you have to make ends meet. It gives you the power to create the life you want for yourself and your family without being held back. It allows you to venture beyond the boundaries of your comfort zone.

One of the negative aspects of wealth is the constant fear of not having enough. Regardless, a persistent feeling of inadequacy about your funds may linger. This fear can hinder you from fully enjoying the fruits of your labor and can lead to a never-ending cycle of accumulation and dissatisfaction. Financial freedom is about breaking free from this fear and finding peace, knowing that you have enough to live in contentment and pursue your dreams.

Once again, wealth is indeed freedom. It is the ability to live on your own terms without worry. This book will guide you on the path to creating this freedom by not only focusing on the accumulation of money, but also helping you build a solid foundation of financial stability. Remember, wealth is not about the number in your bank account, but the sense of peace and freedom that comes with knowing you have the resources to live your desired life. Let this book guide you on the journey to financial freedom, where wealth is truly a gateway to a life of abundance and fulfillment.

In this book, I will discuss two fundamental truths that can lead you on the path to wealth. Creating wealth is simple, though not necessarily easy. The methods and strategies I will outline may be challenging to stick to, but with faith, patience, and discipline, you can overcome any obstacles that come your way. Most investors lack these qualities, which is why they cannot achieve true wealth.

The second fundamental truth is that following the principles and rules I outline will ensure long-term wealth. If you can trust these principles and stay dedicated to your goals, you will eventually see the fruits of your labor and achieve financial success.

It is important to remember that while these truths may seem simple, they require dedication and hard work to see results. You may face setbacks and challenges along the way, but by staying committed and believing, you can overcome any obstacles in your path to wealth.

Ultimately, it is up to you to take control of your financial future and follow the principles that will lead you to success. By staying focused and dedicated to your goals, you can create a pathway to wealth that is both sustainable and fulfilling. Trust, stay faithful to the principles, and wealth will be within your reach.

One more thing:

I wish I could claim that there are quick and easy paths to success, but regrettably, there are not. There is no easy fix. If you are three years away from retirement and have only $250,000 in capital and realize you need $1,000,000 to retire comfortably, neither this book nor anything else can reliably make it happen for you. Not that it is impossible, but highly improbable. Yet, in order to improve the probability of success, you must faithfully follow the lessons found within this book.

Also, consider this adventure like planting a tree. You dig into the earth, plant the sapling, add fertilizer and water and let it grow. You don't dig it up every 30 days to see how it's doing. That is too short a time. Nor do you dig it up when winter comes to protect it in your garage during the bad weather. During the winter, it will stop growing, and the leaves will die, but spring will come and continue to grow again; this is investing. Let it be. You have a plan. You give it enough space, sunlight, time, and prune as required. It will provide shade and beauty for you and your family as it grows.

Creating wealth is just as organic as growing a tree. Growth in the equity markets is no less a force of nature. Remember, wealth is freedom. It frees us from the financial worries you might have now. Wealth provides the freedom to live the life way you wish to. It is distinct from the work you do with the sweat of your brow. Though the principles and methods in this book are simple, there will be times when they will be difficult to stick to. I said they were simple, not necessarily easy. It will require faith, patience and discipline. You can do this.

Let's get digging. Oh, and smile.

"Never let yesterday use up too much of today."

Will Rogers

1. Your Journey Begins.

As you embark on your journey to do better in the markets, remember that you are not alone. I am not just here with you; I am your partner in this journey, cheering you on and guiding you through the trials of the market. It takes courage and determination to take control of your financial future, and I deeply believe in your bravery and potential. While it may seem intimidating at first, remember that no one is more dedicated to your success than you. You have the power to shape your own destiny and create the life you desire. It may be nerve-racking to step into the unknown, but I have full faith in your ability to thrive in the market.

Remember, this is not a get-rich-quick scheme. It takes time, effort, and persistence to see success in the markets. But with dedication and guidance, you can achieve your financial goals and secure a brighter future. So take a deep breath, trust in yourself, and seize control of your destiny. I am here to support you, offer advice, and help you navigate the complexities of the market. Together, we can work towards your goals and ensure your success in the world of trading and investing. I am committed to your success and ready to help you achieve your dreams. Let's do this together and make your financial future a reality.

As a guide, mentor, coach, or student, I believe intimacy and trust are the foundations of any successful relationship. The absence of these crucial components makes it challenging to establish authentic connections and support each other's growth and success. I have spent 45 years working in the financial industry, learning from my own mistakes and experiences along the way. Now, I am here to share my knowledge with you, to help you navigate the markets and avoid the costly pitfalls that I have encountered.

Building a relationship based on intimacy, and trust is crucial for both parties involved. As a mentor, I must be able to open up and share my own experiences, successes, and failures with you. This level of vulnerability allows you to see that I am human, just like you, and that I have made mistakes in the past. It also creates a sense of empathy and understanding between us, which is essential for effective communication and learning. Similarly, as a student, it is important for you to trust in my guidance and expertise. You must listen, learn, and take risks in order to grow and succeed in the financial world.

By building a firm foundation of trust, you can feel confident in my advice and direction, knowing that I have your best interests at heart. Intimacy and trust also contribute to a sense of accountability in our relationship. When you trust in my guidance, you are more likely to follow through on the actions and strategies that I recommend. This level of accountability is key to achieving your financial goals and becoming a successful investor.

These elements are the basis for establishing any beneficial relationship. By fostering these qualities in our mentor-student relationship, we can create a strong foundation for growth, learning, and success. Let me guide you on this journey, sharing my knowledge and experiences, so that you can avoid the costly mistakes that I made and reach your full potential in the market.

In the world of trading and investing, we discover an abundance of strategies and approaches to generate wealth. Each trader or investor has their own unique style and philosophy for making investment decisions. While some may disagree with my approach to trading and philosophy, I am comfortable with the strategies I have developed over the years.

I have spent countless years studying the markets, analyzing trends, and honing my skills as a trader. I have developed a method that works for me and has allowed me to succeed in the markets. My brother and I created the app called Beyond ETFs Pro, which embodies the approach I use and is available in the app store. More information can be found at https://beyondetfspro.com. I also use my approach with my clients in our day-to-day activities.

It's essential to keep in mind that trading does not have a one-size-fits-all approach. What works for one person may not work for another. That is why finding a strategy that aligns with your individual goals, risk tolerance, and investment style is essential. Whether you are a day trader, swing trader, or long-term investor, there is a strategy out there that will work for you.

If my approach to trading does not resonate with you, that is completely fine. I understand everyone has their own unique approach to the markets. I hope that even if you do not agree with my methods, you can still take away something of value from my experiences. Perhaps you will discover a nugget of wisdom that you can apply to your own trading strategy, or maybe you will feel inspired to develop a strategy that better suits your individual needs, the most important thing is to be open-minded and willing to learn from others.

The financial markets constantly evolve, providing endless opportunities for learning. By keeping an open mind and being willing to explore different approaches to trading, you can continue to grow and develop as a trader. Find the approach that works best for you, and don't be afraid to challenge yourself and try new things. Who knows, you may just find a strategy that leads to success beyond your wildest dreams.

A quote attributed to Aristotle goes,

"We are what we repeatedly do. Excellence, then, is not an act but a habit."

I would swear he was talking about investing if I didn't know better. Let me repeat that.

"We are what we repeatedly do. Excellence, then, is not an act but a habit."

However, it's interesting to note that the real origin of this quote is Will Durant, who was simplifying Aristotle's contribution to philosophy. Regardless of its source, the essence remains: **Excellence becomes ingrained when practiced consistently.**

Practicing and repeating any activity we embark upon is necessary for our success. The best athletes do not go out onto the field and wing it. They excel because they dedicate themselves to the discipline of their craft. In baseball, if you fail 70% of the time at bat, you will make it into the Hall of Fame. It is said that Michael Jordon missed 12,345 shots in his career. He was in almost 300 losing games, and he was called upon to take the game-winning shot, but he missed 26 times. [1]

Investing well is not the luck of the draw, a single shot in the dark, or acting on a "tip." It is not a onetime event. It is a repeatable procedure. Investing well is a process. Adaptability is crucial for a disciplined approach. It is possible to learn and, more importantly, replicate this behavior. Understanding the process makes it easy - it just takes practice and insight. It's not complicated. Believe me. I want you to succeed; when you realize your success, everyone around you wins, and we all win. An interesting thing about success is that it's like a breath of air; although your last breath of air is essential, it's not nearly as important as the next. So, let's win together and repeat the process. You can do this, honest.

We must consistently adapt, grow and apply what we learn to succeed at investing.

I found a fascinating article about our perception of the skill sets required for learning. At one point or another in our lives, we all have felt that we could not do that or learn this. For me, it is languages. After attempting grade nine French for the second time, Sister Maria and I came to an understanding. If I promised not to retake it, she would pass me. I kept my word.

Then again, years later, in the winter of 2018, I sent my children a picture of my ID card from the Universidad La Salle in Mexico City and asked them if they could guess what I was doing. They assumed I was teaching. Sadly, no, I was taking a Spanish course. I thundered in on this language attempt as well. Three days before the final exam, it occurred to me I was supposed to be having fun, and

[1] Statmus, https://www.statmuse.com/nba/ask/how-many-missed-shots-did-michael-jordon. Viewed 27 May 2024

I sure wasn't. I stood up and, in broken Spanish, wished everyone success and walked out of the classroom.

After reading the article and reviewing the paper, I have changed my focus from a language butcher to a Spanish student. I already know three essential phases and am learning more.

3.) Dónde queda el baño (where is the bathroom?)

2.) Una taza de café con leche por favor (a cup of coffee with milk, please.)

And the most important one:

1.) Lo siento, mi amor (I am sorry, my dear)

I have this, in part because of Koedinger et al. paper.

In their paper titled "An Astonishing Regularity in Student Learning Rates," Koedinger et al. (2023) state:

"*We find that students are not at mastery at the start of practice, and substantial learning occurs from the practice itself as students receive feedback on their performance and make use of context-sensitive verbal instruction and examples. We find that a typical student needs about seven learning opportunities to master a typical knowledge component.*".

They further state:

The learning rate question is practically important because it bears on fundamental questions regarding education and equity. Can anyone learn to be good at anything they want? Or is talent, like having a "knack for math" or a "gift for language," required? Our evidence suggests that given favourable learning conditions for deliberate practice and given, the learner invests effort in sufficient learning opportunities. ***Indeed, anyone can learn anything they want****. (*my bold*)* [2]

"Research on expertise (Ericsson et al., 1993) indicates that even historic geniuses needed years of practice to develop their expertise. Ericsson (Ericsson, 2008) estimates that high-level expertise takes about 10,000 hours of practice to develop and claims that no substantial exceptions have been found. In other words, no matter who you are, you need many repeated practice opportunities to develop expertise."

I understand you read the part about 10,000 hours of practice and felt tempted to stop reading it and request a refund, but listen to my explanation. You don't need nearly 10,000 hours. I've already done it, and more for you. It would be best if you pulled a Henry Ford. Let me explain.

You Don't Need to Know Everything To Succeed.

Many people feel they must have all the answers to be successful, believing they need to master every aspect. If asked a question they don't know the answer to, they might provide an answer, even if it is incorrect, to avoid looking foolish.

Most of the world's most prosperous people understand that they don't need all the answers to succeed. They may possess specialized knowledge in certain fields, but what is truly important is knowing where to find the answers. Henry Ford proved in his libel

[2] Koedinger, page 18

trial after the First World War that having a solid team of people to rely on is far more important than having all the answers.

An "Ignorant Pacifist"

After World War I, a Chicago paper published articles claiming that Henry Ford was an "ignorant pacifist." Mr. Ford objected to the statements and brought a libel suit against the paper. He took the astonishing move of putting himself on the witness stand to prove that he was not, after all, ignorant.

While on the stand, the attorneys sprayed Henry Ford with questions ranging from "Who was Benedict Arnold?" to "How many soldiers did the British send to America to put down the Rebellion of 1776?" To the last question, he replied: "*I do not know the exact number of soldiers the British sent over, but I have heard that it was a considerably larger number than ever went back.*"

From the line of questioning, Mr. Ford did not know the answers and soon grew tired and weary of the preceding. As the questions became more and more outrageous, Henry Ford pointed his finger at the lawyer who had asked and spoke a simple sentence that floored the court and ended the hearing in an instant:

"If I should really WANT to answer the foolish question, you have just asked or any of the other questions you have been asking me, let me remind you that I have a row of electric push-buttons on my desk, and by pushing the right button, I can summon to my aid men who can answer ANY question I desire to ask concerning the business to which I am devoting most of my efforts. Now, will you kindly tell me WHY I should clutter up my mind with general

knowledge for the purpose of being able to answer questions when I have men around me who can supply any knowledge I require?"[3]

How could we argue against this simple answer from the founder of the Ford Motor Company? Henry Ford did not have all the answers; he could get an answer with the simple push of a button and use this to his advantage to win the day.

You Too Can Be Like Henry Ford

So, let me help you become like Henry Ford.

Another fascinating quote I like from Ford follows:

"The highest use of Capital is not to make more money, but to make money do more for the betterment of Life." - Henry Ford

The question is: What would improve your life? Can you retire worry-free? Are there more vacations planned? Is it more time for your spouse, children, and grandchildren? Is it more for your favorite charity? I don't know what will put a smile on your face or an extra skip in your step, but I can bet you it most likely will involve more money. I would love to help you create a life where you cannot outlive your resources. Your ending account balance is higher each year than your beginning one was after all your withdrawals.

Let's use your money "for the betterment of your life," whatever that entails. Let's do it now, not tomorrow. Smile; you can do this, honest.

[3] McLachlen D, 2014, 'How Henry Ford Proves You Don't Need to Know It All', Lean News, 10 September

***** Spoiler Alert *****

Some people like to jump to the end of the movie or book to find out the ending.

If you can't wait and wish to view the up-to-date results of my work go to:

https://beyondeftspro.com

As a purchaser of my book you can receive monthly updates by emailing me at: wilf@brockmann.com with "Model monthly update" in the subject heading.

2. My Story.

I will share with you what I discovered over my 45-year career as a vice president and investment advisor, first with Merrill Lynch, then with a large retail bank, and finally as a private hedge fund manager. My career spanned from 1980 to 2015 with Merrill and the Bank until a heart attack and a disagreement with the bank's management made me realize parting ways was best for me.

I love the markets. I wanted to help people make money and enjoy buying and selling securities. The financial industry has changed so much for the better since I first started.

In my life, I have found that there are three groups of people who don't appreciate independent thinkers: music conductors, the military, and big businesses. My biggest personal growth was during the Great Recession and after the 2008 market meltdown. In early 2009, at the bottom of the markets, I had my epiphany, my personal discovery on the road to Damascus event. But first, let me tell you a little about myself.

I have always had a passion for the markets. Honest. This was clear from a very young age. My Kindergarten report card from Reed Public School in Arlington, Virginia, reads:

"He is consistent in his actions and participation in group projects, and he leads many projects involving the creation of stores (bakery, drug, food, etc.) and the buying and selling of materials."

By grade 4, I had my insurance company. I provided sickness insurance for my family and the neighborhood. For a nickel premium, I would pay out a quarter if you became sick and had to spend the day at home and a dime for any days thereafter. I was the richest kid in the neighborhood until the altercation.

My sister Barbara got sick at school, and my mother took her to the doctor but returned her to school. That is how I remembered it. She said she stayed home for the day. Time has a way of changing memories, and I am going to say hers, not mine. She misunderstood the contract and broke into my treasury to steal my money. After a brief scuffle, the government intervened (my father) and closed me down. He had been paying the premiums for most of my siblings, anyway.

My next endeavor was Wilfred's Bank. During that time, the law mandated that banks offer a 6% return on all deposits. My brother Peter had just received $10 for a special occasion, and I suggested he deposit it into my bank, and I would pay him 1%. He asked, "What's 1%," I said, "If you had $1,000, I would pay you $10." he looked at his new crisp bill and became the next depositor in Wilfred's Bank. I was playing the interest spread. Shortly afterwards, once again, the government stepped in forcefully, compelling me to relinquish all profits and issuing a fine. It was something about teaching me a lesson. Sure did. Governments need to stay out of the path of business people. Regulators, darn them.

Fast-forward 15 years, and after obtaining a couple of university degrees, Merrill Lynch hired me on October 20, 1980. While in New York, I witnessed a ticker tape parade celebrating the release of the American hostages from Iran. That was so cool. I spent some time training and working in New York City, then finally settled and set up my business in London, Ontario, Canada. In January 1990, Merrill Lynch sold its Canadian retail division to CIBC Wood Gundy. I went over with the furniture, where I stayed until my heart attack in August 2015, and left the firm a short time afterwards.

I love the markets. It is a passion of mine. I want to help people make money. I love buying and selling stocks. Over the past 45 years, I have studied, developed, and proved an investment method, cleverly called the 'Brockmann Method'. This disciplined approach to investing has worked for me and can work for you, too.

As I mentioned, my biggest personal growth was during the Great Recession of 2008—2009. This was the moment of enlightenment, my personal epiphany, and things started to fall into place for me.

The Awakening

I honestly can't remember the exact moment, but the experience has seared itself into my memory. The fog approached gradually, leaving no room for escape. Or that feeling you have when you are driving down the road minding your own business, humming that song when suddenly, the flashing lights in the rearview mirror catch your attention. "It's not for me? It has to be for someone else." Then you look down at your speed and see it is for you.

That awkward feeling when someone catches you with your hands in the cookie jar, and you have no excuse. You know better. You were thinking, sure, I can get out of this market; I see the signs. Yes, the market looks iffy. I have plenty of time. Just a little longer, and this will turn around, please! It's just a correction, right?

WRONG.

That familiar nauseating sensation in the pit of your stomach—the one I experienced in 2002 at the conclusion of the dot-com crisis. The same words you told yourself and your clients: "I will not let this happen to us again." Wrong again. What a disappointment now. I let myself and my clients down for not paying close enough attention.

They say that the definition of insanity is doing the same thing repeatedly, expecting different results. Many investors, including myself, followed a path of listening intently to the suggestions and advice of the "Best Experts" of the day. I no longer do. As we know, 2008 didn't turn out so well for us. Neither did 2000-2002, 1998, 1994 and 1987. Many investors will read the research of noted analysts, economists, and market pundits or key information in the comments of television commentators and their guests. Their work is not part of my process anymore.

How could I have let it happen again? How could I have allowed someone to trick me again? Why didn't I see this? Why was I blinded? The crash of 2008 was different for me, and it was the final straw for me. I was getting older, and my clients were getting older. I really didn't want to go through this all over again. But here we go again! Why me? Why us? I must say I was pretty arrogant.

I remember reading a piece about the subprime mortgage issue in 2004 or 2005 and feeling confident that it was a US issue and pertained only to that market. Then Jérôme Kerviel, the rogue French trader, made headlines in January 2008 when he brought down Société Générale, one of France's major banks. His rogue trades resulted in staggering losses of €4.9 billion. By spring, you had rumors of several money market funds underwater.

I remember reading about Bear Steins' collapse in the terminal after returning from a cruise in March 2008 and spat out my coffee. Then, the unthinkable happened—the bankruptcy of Lehman Brothers on September 15, 2008. I still believed that we would be affected, but again, I thought this was a problem specific to the US and not something that would affect the world.

Then, the next day, AIG gets a bailout. "*There's no place like home; there's no place like home; there's no place like home.*[4]" Until my bank announced it would take a $3 Billion write-down because of subprime mortgages it held. Oh, oh. "*Well, ya got trouble, my friend, right here. I say, trouble right here in River City,*[5]" and it also turns out everywhere.

I lost clients; they just left. I couldn't blame them. I lost everything myself as well. Everything. The "experts" had let us down. I had to take responsibility. I was the guy who had made the recommendations repeatedly. Hold the course. It will get better. I felt betrayed. I felt lower than a snake's belly. I was so low I had to reach up to touch the bottom. The Great Recession caused me to lose everything. I felt I had no credibility, and I didn't. Actually, in my recovery process, I prepared a slide and pinned it on my wall in my office at home that of Scarlett O'Hara's famous cry… "*As God is my witness, I will never let this happen again." OK, so I changed it to suit my situation,* but you get the point.

[4] Vidor, K., Fleming, V., Cukor, G., Thorpe, R., Taurog, N., & LeRoy, M. (1939). *The Wizard of Oz*. Metro-Goldwyn-Mayer (MGM). Segment when Dorothy is clicking her heels in the attempt to get back home to rural Kansas.

[5] Willson, Meredith. "Ya Got Trouble." *The Music Man*, Asylum Records, 1957, track 3.

In the spring of 2009, after the market had bottomed, I remember reading a piece from a writer I had subscribed to. He boasted his portfolio returns had outperformed the markets and were only down -16% during the Great Recession. Mind you, this was a heck of a lot better than me because I was down 20-30+%

I couldn't see myself bragging about losing -16%. It started me thinking, mind you. He was talking about a process he was using called Relative Strength—not the Relative Strength Indicator we all have on our charting packages, but comparing each security in a universe against the others.

It was like an arm wrestling match. It got me thinking. This guy had a long-only portfolio using US EFTs, but I was thinking about reverse EFTs. Why not create a long/short portfolio? He used the same software I used then, so I said what the heck and set about creating my personal recovery. I had nothing to lose.

Uncertainty and the Dart

I was sitting in my office after the market closed, and I glanced over at my TV, which I had on mute, and I noticed a fella was being interviewed. It wasn't the interview that caught my eye but the headline running underneath in the ticker. It said something about Dr. Phillip Tetlock's research. I had come across Tetlock's work before, or I should say I had heard of it and told myself that I would someday go hunting to view it. So here was this guy on TV talking about this. What a break. I unmuted the TV and caught the last part of the interview with Dan Gardner, discussing his new book, *Future Babble.*

In it, Dan discusses why pundits make predictions, why people listen to them, and why you would ultimately be better off with a dart-throwing chimpanzee. Wow, this was a real wake-up call. The fact is that experts are terrible at predictions: We all feel and know that, or maybe just us cynics. On my way home, I made a slight detour and picked up a copy.

In Future Babble, Gardner acknowledges his debt to political scientist Philip Tetlock, who set up a 25-year experiment to investigate the characteristics of a good forecaster.

In Tetlock's study, he considered four factors.

1. He enrolled 286 experts who made their living "commenting or offering advice on political and economic trends." These are the same people whom investment firms and advisory firms employ to read the tea leaves and produce research reports that are sent to clients.

2. Tetlock signed a non-discloser statement in the hopes of more open commentary and less guarded or hedged predictions.

3. He structured the questions in a way that allowed for measuring the outcome. For example, I could say that I predict oil will rise to $200. However, I could not leave the prediction open-ended. My prediction would have to be oil rising to $200 a barrel buy 2026.

4. Forecasters also had to assign probabilities to the outcome. So, if I made a prediction on oil, I would also have to say when and the chances of that occurring. I could predict that oil would reach $200 by 2026, with an 80% probability of obtaining that.

By the end of the study, Tetlock had quantified 82,631 different predictions and later checked how well they performed. To his surprise, Tetlock concluded that "a dart-throwing chimpanzee" would have beaten most of his experts. Not so well for the supposed experts.

Tetlock found that the experts wearing rose-tinted glasses "assigned probabilities of 65 percent to rosy scenarios that materialized only 15 percent of the time." Doomsters did even worse: "They assigned probabilities of 70 percent to bleak scenarios that materialized only 12 percent of the time."

After Tetlock tallied up the data, the predictive failures of the pundits became obvious. Despite being paid for their keen insights into world affairs, they performed worse than random chance. Most of Tetlock's questions had three options for answers; the pundits, on average, selected the right answer less than 33 percent of the time. A dart-throwing chimp would have beaten the vast majority of professionals. Tetlock also found that the least accurate pundits in his study were the most famous or well-known ones, consistently churning out overblown and overconfident forecasts. Eminence was a handicap. Hmmm, it sounds sort of familiar.

After reading his book, I contacted Dan and struck up a dialogue with him about his book and the research he had done. I told him I was a little disappointed that there wasn't a section of the Financial Services Sector.

In my correspondence with Gardner, he wrote to me:

"In my original plan for the book, I had a chapter on financial gurus. Most of it was written, but we dropped it simply to keep the book short, which was necessary, in a practical sense, but also a

shame. Some of the money guys I interviewed -- very big names — were the finest illustrations of the sort of expert we should flee from. But they were confident. Oh lord, were they confident. Absolutely unshakable. No matter what happened, they were right all along. Truly amazing."

I can think of several of them he must have interviewed. Why, then, do people even listen?

Besides mocking the failures of the prognosticating class, Gardner also explains why so many of us keep falling for false prophecy: human beings hate uncertainty. Gardner offers myriad insights from cognitive psychology and behavioral economics research that explain how and why we succumb to our desires for certainty. "*Whether sunny or bleak, convictions about the future satisfy the hunger for certainty,*" writes Gardner. "*We want to believe. And so we do.*"

It's fine, I suppose if you listen to forecasts for entertainment, like the weather or your horoscope. But knowing the track record of forecasters, why in the heck would you ever base your investment policy on a forecast? I'm not talking about just extreme forecasts like the rosy scenario or gloom-and-doom.

A pie chart that allocates assets based on a forecast of expected returns and expected correlations is no less a forecast—and no more likely to be accurate.

That chart of the Efficient Frontier is just as much a forecast as anything else your advisor may present to you. My question is: Whose data are they using, and what time frame? The curve will change over time, which is not good if your retirement plan hinges on this data.

I am not in the business of making predictions; rather, I am in the business of identifying market leadership and adapting to changes along the way. I will explain how later.

"Prediction is very difficult, especially about the future." Niels Bohr

Here is a letter I came across dated 12 January 2013, which I sent out to clients. It speaks to the guru class of pundits and their track record. The facts still bear out today:

Dear:

No wonder the average investor is dazed and confused. I came across an article in the Wall Street Journal on Thursday, December 27, 2012, entitled *2012 Was Good for Stocks, Bad for Stock Pundits*. The article reviewed the track record for some well-known market pundits. After detailing some of the blown 2012 calls by Jim Rogers and Jim Cramers, the article provides the following rather dreary summary:

... Neither Mr. Rogers nor Mr. Cramer should feel singled out. The business of market punditry is fraught with potholes.

Of the 65 market "gurus" tracked during the last few years by CXO Advisory Group, the median accuracy for market calls is 47%. If that sounds low, or you wonder about the quality of the pundit, consider that the list includes such well-known names as Bill Fleckenstein (37%), Jeremy Grantham (48%), Bill Gross (46%) and Louis Navellier (60%).

The record speaks for itself. Most of the smartest guys in the room are usually about as reliable as a coin flip. After the bombing in 2011 with a prediction that Treasury yields would rise, Mr. Gross, founder and co-chief investment officer of Pacific Investment Management Co., didn't make any sweeping predictions for 2012 except to say he worried about Europe."

Something to keep in mind while reviewing forecasts for 2013. In this light, I use Relative Strength as a guide to help me detect strength as well as avoid weakness. It's not a predicative tool, but we know that securities that are strong continue being strong, and those that are weak continue being weak. This year I will strive to heed the advice of Albert Einstein: **"A man should look for what is, and not for what he thinks should be".** Who knew he was talking about Relative Strength?

Sincerely,

Wilf

"Isn't it strange? The same people who laugh at gypsy fortune tellers take economists seriously."—Cincinnati Enquirer.

I will speak about Relative Strength and how I employ it along with the Einstein quote later on.

Here is another piece from the crypt that I came across. You find an amassing amount of information when you go through your files.

Do as I Say, Not as I Do?

January 10, 2011

Hmmm..it seems that the better way in the financial markets is to pay attention to what price is doing—and to ignore what the analysts say. As per Bloomberg,

.... Following the advice of equity analysts may be perilous for your profits. Companies in the Standard & Poor's 500 Index that analysts loved the most rose 73 percent on average since the benchmark for US equity started to recover in March 2009, while those with the fewest "buy" recommendations gained 165 percent, according to data compiled by Bloomberg.

Despite this, investors still pay attention to research reports and CNBC. We believe your time is better spent on a systematic examination of relative strength, which is what I do.

I had completely forgotten about these facts. I had stopped watching the business channels long ago because I realized they were not my friend. They are trying to sell a product. The product is advertising space. Just consider the news channels now.

Wilf

"An economist is an expert who will know tomorrow why the things he predicted yesterday didn't happen today." Laurence J Peter.

Game Day

I look at investing in a way similar to the game of football. Each Sunday, you'll see your favorite team's coach pacing the sidelines, holding a laminated "playbook," and sometimes even throwing it. The team spends the entire week compiling a catalogue of plays to use against their opponents, based on variables such as field position and whether they are on offense or defense.

Why shouldn't we do the same thing?

As your advisor, you have hired me to coach your investment team and to be the most effective coach possible; it means having a Playbook, a catalogue of plays we are comfortable implementing depending on the situation—whether on offence with excellent field position, offence with poor field position, defense, etc. Having a playbook established ahead of time lets us focus more objectively when the time comes, hopefully enabling us to fight some emotions that will misdirect us at any time. We don't want to react to the noise from the crowd or the "experts" on TV. Let's concentrate on the game and the things happening on the field.

We want to play our game and act appropriately.

The Playbook

Of course, any football coach must know two important things when deciding on what particular play to run:

Should the offensive or defensive team be on the field? And what is my field position?

This is true for us, too, as we decide which investment strategy or play to run. So this leads us to the best way to answer this all-important initial question.

But before that, we want to lead today's discussion with an overview of the Four-Step Game Plan for Investing. This game plan is the backbone of our recommended risk management method and will permeate the building of our playbook. It is a top-down approach, focusing first on analyzing the overall market and then determining sector opportunities because this is where most risk lives in any stock (based on a University of Chicago study). From there, we build our fundamental inventory of ideas and finish the process by technically analyzing this sound list of ideas. For the Beyond ETFs Pro program, we use the S&P 100 universe to choose which team members to put on the team.

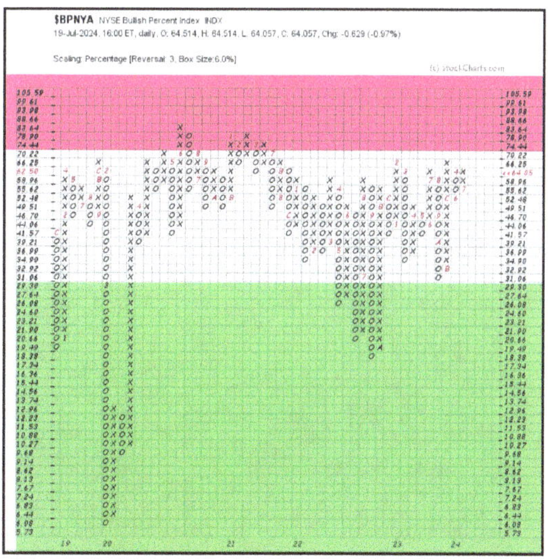

Basically, we are dealing with Step One of the Game Plan. This step answers the two questions we posed at the start: Offense or Defense? And what is my field position?

In building our Playbook, we must always start by answering those two questions as that will determine which plays we should implement depending on whether we are on Offense or Defense and whether you are in the Green Zone (lower risk environment), the middle of the field, or in the Red Zone (higher risk territory).

The process of selecting our investment strategy and managing our trades depends on our field position, and whether on offense or defense. We can apply different strategies for both entry and exit.

So, where are we in the game? Today, we are in center field, and we have just recovered the ball and called the offensive team onto the field. The market has given us the ball and we are in wealth creation mode. We will focus on some plays found in the yellow top portion of the playbook. I will explain how we determine the field position later, so for now, sit back and enjoy the game. I have a few plays to review. To access the most current data, visit https://beyondetfspro.com and navigate to the tabs for our numbers.

3. At the Crossroad.

Our hunger for certainty does not guarantee its availability.

The only thing I can predict with any certainty is that things will continue to change unpredictably. I also don't know what the market will do next, but I know what I will do.

Following a closer examination and pondering of the Tetlock study and others, I realized I should be very careful with the advice offered by "Experts." I stopped reading all the research reports provided to me. The rookies loved it when I would go around handing off all the reports gathered on my desk. I stopped watching the business news channels. This freed up an enormous amount of time and energy. And it felt incredibly liberating. In the past, I would have picked over the tea leaves offered by the analysts to gain an advantage in understanding a situation. I would stress over things I had no control over. I still stress a little, but not as much now.

This next event occurred in February. Not feeling well, I left work around noon to rest most of the afternoon. At around 3:30, I thought I would turn on the TV rather than turn on my computer to check the markets. As the minutes passed, I found myself getting more and more engrossed in their conversation, as if it held great significance. I became more hypnotized by the siren's call. Ah, that irresistible, haunting melody that lures sailors and investors toward the rocky shores.

I finally jumped up, turned off the TV, and saved my soul. OK, it's a little over the top, but they are only commentators with their own message based on who knows what. Really, what value do they bring to the table if they lean each way the wind blows? We forget these commentators are not our friends. They have a product to sell, and that is to drive advertising revenue.

People spend too much time watching or reading their latest guru for their take on the current investment environment. This is their most accurate prediction of future events, though it remains purely conjectural. The complexities of today's global markets require a foundation built on more than just opinion. Opinion is too primitive a tool to deal with today's global markets, which are constantly changing! Objectivity is required to wade through the mind-numbing bits of data to isolate the most important variable in the investment process, which is the supply/demand relationship.

In today's complex and fast-moving world, information is spinning at us at an ever-faster pace, making it hard to make sense of it all. The major flaw in the traditional investment paradigm used by the vast majority of investors is their dependence upon someone else's "subjective analysis," "predictions & forecasts," and "personal opinions."

I remember once being at a client presentation where the keynote speaker was the Deputy Chief Economist of our bank. He recounted a tale of catching the red-eye flight back from Regina, Saskatchewan, amid the February frigid cold. During the flight, he contemplated whether to finish the report he planned on publishing or to take a break and complete it the next morning at the office. He tossed and turned and finally did it. Basically, he completed the calculations on the back of the proverbial envelope. He plugged them into the formula and rested the remaining flight.

A few weeks later, while reading a report published by the Bank of Canada (BOC), he discovered with joy that his figure aligned with the BOC's figure. Well, they had much more resources to devote to this issue than he had, and he had done it at 30,000 feet. A short while later, while in discussion with one of the Deputy Directors of the BOC, about 45 minutes into the discussion, he asked them how they came up with their figures. The Director hummed and hauled and, when pressed, finally admitted they had used his numbers! I stopped attending these functions, and no longer invited clients. I didn't want them to be confused.

Red pill or blue pill?

In The Matrix, the hero, Neo, faces a choice that ultimately changes the course of his life when offered a red or blue pill. The red pill, symbolizing the journey of self-discovery and uncovering the truth, breaks the illusion of the simulated world and brings Neo to the existing harsh reality, to the state of what is, no matter how uncomfortable or challenging it may be. The blue pill represents remaining ignorant, living in the comforting illusion, and following the status quo. Believing what you are told to believe.

As I contemplate my experiences, this concept resonated with me. Like Neo, I, too, accepted the metaphorical red pill. I became disillusioned with mindlessly following the advice of so-called experts and advisors who seemed to have all the answers yet presented us with poor results. I saw through the constructed facade. Refusing to follow the crowd down a path that did not align with my values or beliefs. This disconnect grew wider as time went on. I realized I was capable of independent thought and decision-making instead of relying solely on the guidance of others. And like in The Wizard of Oz, I discovered that a mere mortal was pulling the levers behind the curtain.

I began questioning their motives and agendas, realizing their guidance was not always in my or my client's best interest. As I distanced myself from their influence, I discovered a newfound sense of independence in my thoughts and decisions. However, this newfound independence and confidence left me feeling adrift, much like Neo in the desert, with no clear direction.

Thus began the adventure. I couldn't rely on the "Experts.". They had been entirely wrong, and I was finally realizing that they were also clueless. It didn't matter what the CEO of the company or the analysts said; they were only guesses at the best of times. At least in my mind. You may have similar feelings.

So here I am, as a professional money manager, challenging everything I was taught and grew up believing. I was at a loss. I was at a crossroads and didn't know which path to take.

I sought alternative sources of information and advice, looking beyond the mainstream narratives and conventional wisdom. I embraced the uncertainty and challenges that came with being an independent thinker in a world that often rewards conformity and complacency. As I continued down this path of self-discovery, I saw the benefits of thinking for myself and making informed decisions based on my research and analysis. I no longer felt the need to rely on others for validation or guidance, trusting in my judgment and instincts instead. This newfound sense of empowerment and autonomy has been liberating, allowing me to navigate the complex world of investing with confidence and clarity.

Taking the red pill meant stepping outside of my comfort zone and facing the unknown. It meant questioning the status quo and exploring alternative paths. It meant being willing to challenge the conventional wisdom and forge my way. As I embraced this newfound independence, I was no longer content to follow the herd simply; I wanted to carve out my path and make informed decisions based on my research and analysis. I was no longer willing to be swayed by the opinions of others, even if they came from seemingly reputable sources.

By embracing independence in thought and decision-making, we can uncover the truth and chart our own course towards success and fulfillment. I am grateful for the red pill moment that opened my eyes to a new way of thinking and living, and I am committed to continuing this journey of self-discovery with courage and conviction.

I had to take risks and make mistakes in order to grow and learn. Yet, my epiphany occurred amid this period of uncertainty. Moments of sheer panic washed over me, but then clarity struck. I realized that if I couldn't trust the experts, then who could I depend on? It all came down to one thing - supply and demand. It became apparent to me I needed to forge my path to take control of my financial future and decision-making process. This realization marked a turning point in my journey toward self-discovery. I educated myself on different and alternative investment strategies and their impact on the financial markets and industry trends.

In the end, taking the red pill was the best decision I could have made. It opened my eyes to new possibilities and allowed me to discover my truth. So, I urge you to take the red pill and embrace your own journey of self-discovery. Trust yourself, question the status quo, and be willing to seek the truth, no matter how uncomfortable it may be. Only then can you break free from the illusions of the world and find your own genuine path.

Why do we always have to complicate things when simple will do? Leonardo da Vinci said it best.

"Simplicity is the ultimate sophistication,"

- Leonardo da Vinci.

Economics 101 - Supply and Demand

Supply and demand are fundamental economic concepts that are crucial in determining the prices and quantities of goods and services in any market. This relationship is the backbone of the market economy, influencing various economic decisions and outcomes. We decide about these functions every day without fully knowing.

During the COVID-19 pandemic, people deemed toilet paper to be of extra value and rushed out to stock up on the product, causing shortages. Governments said they would crack down on price gouging, so shortages sprang up everywhere. Otherwise, prices would have spiked higher. Lettuce prices increase during winter months in Canada as there is no domestic market. One year, drought conditions in California curtailed the supply, causing the prices to spike until a new seasonal crop from Mexico came online. Determining which route we take to get home from work is a function of supply and demand. We may choose another route if a particular route experiences heavy traffic. We have a choice.

Politicians are so silly (can I also say, stupid?) Senator Elizabeth Warren from Massachusetts once outlined a policy in which she proposed that, because of rising food prices, she would have grocery store executives paraded in front of a senate panel if a particular item rose by a specific percentage to explain themselves. The impact of such a policy would be that should a particular item reach close to the stated percentage increase, the grocery chain would stop carrying that item. Why endure the wrath of misinformed politicians and the ensuing PR nightmare? The same goes for toilet paper; let the market determine the price and value. If you need it, you will pay for it. If not, switch to another product. In these cases, we have a massive misallocation of resources.

So, how do we gauge the value of a stock in the stock market?

The fundamental analyst will use various measures, such as P/E ratios, sales forecasts, earning growth, price-to-earnings growth, price-to-book value, and debt ratios, to name just a few. A company's balance sheet or income statement figures can be tampered with; we have many examples of such a thing. Enron (2001), WorldCom (2002), Lehman Brothers (2008), Waste Management and Bernie Madoff all hit the top ten list. Also, scouring the financial figures can lead to a subjective judgement of the company's affairs. If they are subjective, they become subject to interpretation. If subject to interpretation, then whose figures and why those figures?

How do I determine the value of a stock in the stock market? By price, that's how. Price is the final arbitrator. It doesn't matter what the analyst, or the company says. All that matters is the price. The price will eventually incorporate all the commentary and reactions of participants. I realized that "Price" represents a market's best guess about what might happen down the road, rightly or wrongly. Price is an informed guess; people are putting real money on the line. It is the wisdom of the crowd. And again, like da Vinci said, simplicity is the ultimate sophistication. Besides, it is a little more difficult to manipulate IBM or Apple's price action.

Price leaves the investor with a picture of the chart action, and we discuss that in greater detail later in the book.

The Challenger Disaster

Tuesday, January 28, 1986, started like any other day in London, Ontario. Like the other days that month, the weather had an overcast sky. Cold, it had dropped to 2 F (-16 c.) by 09:30 a.m. Nothing was special about the start of the day; it would end differently.

The Dow Jones Industrial Average rose steadily from mid-September to 1,300 and opened that morning at 1,537. Then, mid-morning, it happened. Similar to the Star Wars movie, a force disturbance occurred. We didn't know what, but something was off. The bid/ask spreads widened, and there was a momentary downward plunge. There was no internet or social media. All we had was the Dow Jones wire for contact and news from the outside world.

On January 28, 1986, at 11:38 am, the space shuttle Challenger embarked on its journey from Cape Canaveral. Seventy-four seconds into the flight, at ten miles high, tragedy struck. The pilot's last words, "Challenger go with throttle up," then the shuttle exploded.

The televised launch meant news of the disaster spread rapidly, sparking initial confusion. News hit the Dow Jones News Wire at 11:47 A.M.

Speculation swirled for weeks, attributing the accident to various causes, including a flame on the solid booster rocket. President Reagan appointed a commission to investigate, featuring luminaries like Neil Armstrong and Richard Feynman.

Finally, on June 6, 1986, after over five months, the commission determined the explosion resulted from the failure of the shuttle's infamous O-rings on the right solid fuel booster rocket, pointing the finger at Morton Thiokol, one of NASA's contractors.

The stock market's reaction, however, was swift and merciless. Within minutes of the explosion, investors began shedding shares of the four major contractors involved: Rockwell International, Lockheed, Martin Marietta, and Morton Thiokol and Thiokol suffered the most, with its stock plummeting rapidly caused by of an overwhelming number of sell orders that forced trading to be halted.

By the market close, Thiokol's stock had plummeted nearly 12 percent, while the other contractors experienced lesser declines, with their stocks gradually rebounding by the end of the day.

This immediate market response effectively blamed Morton Thiokol for the disaster despite no public comments singling them out on the day of the tragedy. The faulty O-rings, compromised by cold weather in Florida, allowed hot exhaust gases to escape, sealing Thiokol's fate in the eyes of the market. Still, the market had yet to know that information.

A panel of experts took 6 months to determine that Morton Thiokol was to blame. The market came to the same conclusion within an hour.

Table 1
Daily stock market behavior around the challenger crash

Variable	Morton Thiokol	Lockheed	Martin Marietta	Rockwell International
Panel A. Daily stock returns				
January 28	– 11.86%	– 2.14%	– 3.25%	– 2.48%
3-Month average	0.21%	0.07%	0.14%	0.06%
3-Month standard deviation	1.86%	1.36%	1.79%	1.79%
Z statistic	6.49	1.63	1.89	1.42
Panel B. Daily trading volume				
January 28	1739.9	667.5	446.2	563.2
3-Month average	100.5	347.9	199.9	221.2
3-Month standard deviation	59.5	159.4	136.5	117.1
Z statistic	27.57	2.00	1.80	2.92

This table compares the stock returns and trading volume of the four major space-shuttle firms on January 28, 1986, the day of the Challenger crash, to averages of the same variables in the 3 months (October 28, 1985 to January 27, 1986) prior to the crash. Trading volume is in thousands of shares. *Z* statistics test the null that the observation on January 28 equals the average from the prior 3 months. Data are taken from the *S&P Daily Stock Price Record*.

456 M.T. Maloney, J.H. Mulherin / Journal of Corporate Finance 9 (2003) 453–479

Table 1
Daily stock market behavior around the challenger crash

Variable	Morton Thiokol	Lockheed	Martin Marietta	Rockwell International
Panel A. Daily stock returns				
January 28	– 11.86%	– 2.14%	– 3.25%	– 2.48%
3-Month average	0.21%	0.07%	0.14%	0.06%
3-Month standard deviation	1.86%	1.36%	1.79%	1.79%
Z statistic	6.49	1.63	1.89	1.42
Panel B. Daily trading volume				
January 28	1739.9	667.5	446.2	563.2
3-Month average	100.5	347.9	199.9	221.2
3-Month standard deviation	59.5	159.4	136.5	117.1
Z statistic	27.57	2.00	1.80	2.92

This table compares the stock returns and trading volume of the four major space-shuttle firms on January 28, 1986, the day of the Challenger crash, to averages of the same variables in the 3 months (October 28, 1985 to January 27, 1986) prior to the crash. Trading volume is in thousands of shares. *Z* statistics test the null that the observation on January 28 equals the average from the prior 3 months. Data are taken from the *S&P Daily Stock Price Record*.

Table 1.1.
Stock price movements and returns of the four major space-shuttle firms in the period immediately surrounding the 11:39 a.m. crash of the Space Shuttle *Challenger* on January 28, 1986

Time	Morton Thiokol	Lockheed	Martin Marietta	Rockwell International
Panel A. Stock price movements				
11:30 a.m.	US$37.25	US$47.25	US$35.38	US$34.75
Noon	Halt	US$44.50	US$34.25	US$32.75
12:36 p.m.	US$35.00	US$45.00	US$32.50	US$34.13
1:00 p.m.	US$34.38	US$45.00	US$33.00	US$33.25
Panel B. Stock returns				
11:30–Noon	Halt	−5.82%	−3.18%	−5.76%
Noon–12:36	−6.04%	1.12%	−5.11%	4.20%
12:36–1:00	−1.79%	0.00%	1.54%	−2.56%

Note: There is no reported price for Morton Thiokol at noon because of an NYSE trading halt in that stock from 11:52 a.m. to 12:44 p.m. The first postcrash trade in Morton Thiokol occurred at 12:36 p.m. on NASDAQ.
Source: Maloney and Mulherin (2003, table 2).

Wisdom of the crowd

In his book Wisdom of the Crowd, James Surowiecki describes the story of Sir Francis Galton attending a county fair in the fall of 1906[6]. Sir Galton's interest in the theory of eugenics contributed to his fame. He believed that selective parenthood could improve the human species. Individuals inherit their intellect from birth. "*Galton defended the claim that psychological abilities and tendencies were inherited along with physical characteristics and were thus subject to national selection.*"[7] At this time, debate was raging in the House of Lords about whether to expand the vote to the average person. Given what, Sir. Galton believed and had written on, that he was dead against it. That was about to change.

Among Sir. Galton's hobbies and interests besides statistics were animal husbandry. He was interested in improving the

[6] Surowiecki, James, 2004, *The Wisdom of Crowds : Why the many are smarter than the few and how collective wisdom shapes business, economies, societies, and nations,* Doubleday,
[7] Sweeney, g., 2001, 'Fighting for the Good Cause: Reflections on Francis Galton's Legacy to American Hereditarian Psychology'. American Philosophical Society, 2001. Pp. 136

breeding stock of the herds in England. As he wandered amongst the fair stalls that day, he encountered a weight-judging competition. [8] People were lining up to wager on the dead dressing of an ox. The participants cast Eight hundred ballots, with only 787 being submitted, and 13 were discarded as illegible. He figured that many were farmers or butchers but many were non-experts.

Sir Galton was instantly interested in this endeavor. He could see the parallel between it and democracy's attributes. Here, you had people of various backgrounds with unique abilities, interests, and insights, each with a vote. In the Nature's scientific journal, he would later write, "*like those clerks and others who have no expert knowledge of horses, but who bet on races, guided by newspapers, friends, and their own fancies.*" "*The average competitor was probably as well fitted for making a just estimate of the dressed weight of the ox, as an average voter is of judging the merits of most political issues on which he votes," he* wrote. [9]

Galton wanted to prove that the average voter could not render a proper verdict. After completing the contest, he gathered the ballots and arranged them from the lowest to the highest estimate. He figured that with such a mix of a very few smart, knowledgeable voters, a lot of dumb people, and many mediocre voters, you would end up with a dumb answer, yet he would find himself off the mark.

After slaughtering and dressing the ox, it weighed 1,198 pounds.

The average of all the guesses - 1,197.

[8] Surowiecki, pp.5
[9] Surowiecki, pp.6

Sir Galton would later write, *"The result seems more creditable to the trustworthiness of a democratic judgment than might have been expected."*[10]

Thus, we have the phenomenon of, "The Wisdom of the Crowds.

[10] Surowiecki, pp.6

4. Corner Stone of the Puzzle -1.

There is nothing more difficult to take into hand, more

perilous to conduct, *or more uncertain in its success than*

to take the lead in the introduction of a new order of things.

- Niccolo Machiavelli

"Successful investing demands the confidence and arrogance to strike out independently with the openness and humility to embrace and adapt to superior ideas from others.

– Wilf Brockmann

For me, the old order was passing away. Welcome to the new paradise.

Let's recap what we have discovered so far. By the bottom of the market in the Great Recession of 2008, I could no longer, in good conscience, follow the advice of the "experts." The financial services industry was moving towards a fee-based platform. That way, they got paid in the good times and also in the bad times. I am reminded of an old trading floor saying about options: "*The brokerage firm makes money, the broker makes money; two out of three isn't bad."*

I imagine that under a fee-based regime, the advisor might feel tempted to relax their approach to the risk profile in order to avoid upsetting the apple cart. To ease off the gas pedal and let things float along with everyone else. I am sure many advisors do not succumb to this temptation. I did not want to have that temptation presented to me. My approach has always been that when the client succeeds, I succeed, and when the client suffers, I suffer. I just found that the client relationship would go a lot better if we were sitting on the same side of the table.

I am reminded of a couple of financial cartoons. In the first one, an advisor talks with the investor and said, "*Let's see if we can come up with a plan to send my kids to college.*" Or the other one in which the advisor told the investor, "*For a 1% annual fee, I will invest your money with a certified financial planner. He'll charge 1% per year to put your money in mutual funds that charge 1% per year.*" The investor then said, *"Will I make any money?"* to which the advisor said, "*I don't see you doing any of the work.*"

Technology and its exponential growth have forever changed how individuals interface and interact with the financial markets. Individual's speed of information access is mind-blowing. Costs have shrunk to give individual investors access to previously restricted products.

Speaking of costs and commissions, I am reminded of a presentation given to the local Investors Dealers Association by a Merrill Lynch broker from Princeton in the early 1980s. We had about 14-16 small brokerage shops in London, Ontario. We invited the broker to talk to us about negotiated commissions, what to expect, and how to deal with this new environment. What struck me was not the speech about commissions but his warning about the future of the financial securities industry itself. He warned us about the eventual entry into the brokerage business of the banks. The cultural differences are profound and would have a transformative effect on all of us. He said it would be like a small beer fridge placed in a big room, expecting to cool the room. The small fridge may succeed for a while but will, over time, not be up to the task and will break down. That is precisely what has happened.

EUREKA!!

Since I no longer trusted the pronouncements of the analyst community, economists, market pundits, television commentators, and their guests, I soon discovered I was on my own. Yet, a picture taken from price discovery, the lessons gleaned from the Challenger crash, and the collective intelligence of the masses were all at play. I started studying and researching momentum and other aspects dealing with supply and demand and the key driving forces behind price movements.

In 2010, I came across a research paper that was the EUREKA moment for me. Dr. Tobias J. Moskowitz published his paper, Momentum Investing, Finally Accessible for Individual Investors. [11] In it, he states:

"*Momentum is the tendency of investments to exhibit persistence in their relative performance. Investments that have performed relatively well continue to perform relatively well; those that have performed relatively poorly continue to perform relatively poorly. Momentum investing, however, involves more than buying a handful of hot stocks. It is a disciplined, systematic investing style that applies across asset classes.*

Momentum investing calls for identifying securities with good relative performance in rising, neutral, and falling markets and tries to predict which of those securities will continue to outperform

[11] Moskowitz, T.J, 2010, 'Momentum Investing Finally Accessible for Individual Investors', Investments & Wealth Monitor, Investment Management Consultants Association,

regardless of market trend. Momentum, however, is not a pure trend-following strategy. It makes no bets on rising or falling markets; it works whether markets are trending up or down. [12]

... But assets that have performed well over the past 6-12 months tend to do better over the next 6-12 months than assets that have performed poorly over that same past period. This is the time horizon in which momentum works best."[13]

Possible Explanations for Momentum

Momentum has several explanations. Momentum's higher returns may be a compensation for a unique risk associated with investments that have recently outperformed, though no such risk factor has been convincingly identified. If momentum is not compensation for risk, its existence seems to challenge even the weakest form of the efficient-market hypothesis that past price performance provides no information about future performance. Momentum may be associated with a market inefficiency, perhaps one because of investor behavior.

Several possible behavioral explanations have been put forth, many based on the Nobel Memorial prize-winning work of Daniel Kahneman and Amos Tversky. One explanation posits that investors may be slow to react to new information. Different investors (e.g., a trader vs. a casual investor) receive news from different sources and react to news over different time horizons and in different ways. This "anchoring and adjustment" is a behavioral phenomenon in which individuals update their views only partially when faced with new information, slowly accepting its full impact. Ample evidence supports slow-reaction-to-information theories ranging from

[12] Moskowitz, pp. 1
[13] Moskowitz, pp. 3

market response to earnings and dividend announcements to analysts' reluctance to update their forecasts.

Second, human beings—and therefore, investors—are prone to what behavioral economists and experimental psychologists call the disposition effect. Investors tend to sell winning investments prematurely to lock in gains and hold on to losing investments too long in the hope of breaking even. The disposition effect creates an artificial headwind: When good news is announced, the price of an asset does not immediately rise to its true value because of premature selling or lack of buying. Similarly, when bad news is announced, the price falls less because investors are reluctant to sell. Research shows a strong tendency toward the disposition effect among individual investors (Odean 1998, Grinblatt and Han 2005), Treasury bond traders (Coval and Shumway 2005), and even mutual fund managers (Frazzini 2006).

The debate about the root causes of momentum continues. A similar debate is ongoing for value investing. Evidence from a range of markets, asset classes, and time periods, however, supports the argument that momentum is not random.[14]

Over the years, I have read countless papers, books, and articles dealing with relative strength/ momentum (many use these words interchangeably, as do I) and as much on the subject as possible, including endless combinations and permutations. I assume you might be familiar with these topics or subject points and may gloss over them with little or no explanation, assuming you understand. I am truly sorry and will attempt to explain as much as possible.

Before we proceed, I must confess—I am a relative strength and momentum zealot. My passion for this subject drives me to share

[14] Moskowitz, pp. 3

this knowledge with you to save you from potential pitfalls. But fear not—I will step down from my pulpit and approach our discussion with humility. Now, let's dive back into the world of relative strength and momentum.

The term 'relative' is important for explanation's sake. Momentum and trend following are occasionally mistaken for one another. They have a relationship, but they are not the same. The relative strength process I use ranks securities relative to their peers, while trend following often focuses only on the absolute price changes. Trends following systems will increase exposure during upswings and decrease exposure during downswings. Relative strength does not take a stance on market direction, up or down. It reevaluates securities again in relation to each other. You will find winners and losers in both an up market and a down market. Some say that momentum is the phenomenon where securities that are performing well relative to their peers (they are winners) will, on average, continue to outperform. Stocks that have been underperforming (i.e., the losers) will likely continue to do so.

In the esteemed paper, 'Fact, Fiction, and Momentum Investing', the authors methodically outline and then debunk many of the myths about momentum. This paper is regarded by many for its comprehensive research and analysis. It's a well-established fact, supported by empirical evidence spanning over 212 years from 1801 to 2012 that momentum operates consistently across various asset classes and countries. Despite this, some still harbor doubts, so here is their list of myths.

Myth #1. Momentum returns are too "small and sporadic."

Momentum's existence is hard to deny, and its presence and what I would call robustness have remained stable alongside other factors being studied. Not that it does not have periods of underperformance like everything else in life. Many studies show that Momentum has larger gross returns and Sharpe ratios than both value and size.[15] (Sorry, the economist in me is coming out. I will try to contain these outbreaks.) Like the authors, I am left wondering what the meaning of small means is since momentum exhibits superior numbers when reviewing risk-adjusted returns.

With the growing popularity of momentum strategies, I can see that the perception of shrinking gains will diminish over time, yet that has not been the case. The returns continue to be robust over time despite this growing popularity. I will go into further detail about why individuals may not adopt this relative strength later.

Myth #2. "Momentum can only be exploited on the short side," so long-only investors cannot capture it.

While Jess Livermore and others made significant profits on the short side of the market, it's crucial to acknowledge that one can also make substantial gains from the long side. Israel and Moskowitz's comprehensive analysis of 86 years of US data revealed that momentum's long and short sides are equally lucrative. [16] This finding debunks the myth that momentum can only be exploited on the short side. My experience also collaborates with the authors.

Myth #3: Momentum is much stronger among small-cap stocks than large-caps.

I am tempted to pull out the "Liar, Liar, Pants of Fire" clause on this one. The paper's authors suspect the fans of value investing

15

16 Israel, R., Moskowitz, T. "*The Role of Shorting, Firm Size, and Time on Market Anomalies.*" Journal of Financial Economics, Vol. 108, No. 2 (2013a), pp. 275-301

primarily generated this myth. I am not a fan of value. It makes little sense to me. A value investor will say that the intrinsic value of a stock is $150, but the market is pricing it at $100. The value investor will buy it at $100, knowing that eventually, the market will realize the mis-pricing, and it will rise to the $150 area. My rebuttal to this thought is coming later.

Israel and Moskowitz (2013a) cover extensive work to disprove this myth. From my experience, while running a program with small caps, it greatly underperformed a program of large caps running in tandem. For everything, there is a season.

Myth #4: Momentum does not survive or is severely limited by trading costs.

The question arises: Do the transactional costs reduce momentum's premium? Granted, momentum is a higher turnover strategy than other strategies, such as value, yet trading costs have been driven down, making this a moot point. It might have been years ago, but not now. In their paper "Trading Costs of Asset Pricing Anomalies,"[17] the authors viewed over a trillion dollars of live trades across 19 developed equity markets from 1998 to 2013. Trading costs have since continued downward. They concluded that trading cost per trade was low thus disproving this myth.

Myth #5: Momentum does not work for a taxable investor.

This does not mean it will lead to higher taxes despite the prospects for a higher turnover rate than other strategies. One consideration is that part of the momentum strategy is tax-effective. Yes, it may seem counterintuitive, but consider this:

[17] Frazzini, A., R. Israel, and T.J. Moskowitz. "*Trading Costs of Asset Pricing Anomalies*." Working paper, University of Chicago, 2013

These strategies will sell losers quicker and hold the winners, pushing them into a more favorable tax position. You end up creating short-term losses and having long-term capital gains. On the other hand, value strategies, even while they are holding long-term capital gains, have more dividend income in their portfolios, which in many tax regimes is tax inefficient. All this does is not consider strategies specifically optimized for their tax position. Momentum survives the tax burden, which is comparable to a smaller and lower turnover rate strategy of the likes of value.

Nice try, myth spreader, but you have been busted on this one.

MYTH NO. 6: MOMENTUM IS BEST USED WITH SCREENS RATHER THAN AS A DIRECT FACTOR.

I find this myth strange since if you bad-mouth or demean one strategy, why would you employ it to create another? When someone uses momentum as a shield, they perceive it as a factor that is comparable to value or size. It is, or it isn't. You can't have it both ways. You cannot exhale and inhale simultaneously. Frazzini et al., in their paper, show that a factor-based approach is significantly superior to a screen-based approach.

For myself, I screen various security lists, indexes, or universes of securities to create a list of the strongest and the weakest. Knowing the list of the strongest is just as important as a list of the weakest to avoid. For example, say I want to review the energy sector. I would take a list of all the securities in that index or ETF and rank them using relative strength.

Here is another example of where I use relative strength to screen and rank a list of securities. In their paper, George, and

Hwang [18] discuss their finding of superior returns employing securities at or near their 52-week high. Building upon the study by Liu, Liu, and Ma, the researchers discovered the following results.

Conclusion:

"George and Hwang (2004) find that an investing strategy based on the nearness to the past 52-week high generates comparable profits as the momentum strategy proposed by Jegadeesh and Titman (1993) and the Moskowitz and Grinblatt (1999) industrial momentum strategy in the US market, and these profits do not revert in the long run. In this paper, we conduct a comprehensive study on this 52-week high momentum strategy in 20 major stock markets.

Our main findings are as follows. First, we find that the 52-week high momentum profits are robust in international stock markets. Eighteen out of twenty markets in our sample present evidence of a profitable 52-week high momentum strategy, with ten having significantly positive profits.

...Consistent with George and Hwang (2004), we find that the 52-week high as a price level is a better predictor of future stock returns than macroeconomic risk factors or the acquisition price. It has predictive power no matter whether stocks have had extreme past returns or in the extreme industries.".

[18] George, T., Hwang, CY., *'The 52-Week High and Momentum Investing"*, The Journal of Finance, Vol LIX, NO. 5, October 2004.

I will show an example of a model using a 52-week high list then ranking them using relative strength later in the chapter entitled putting it all together.

MYTH NO. 7: The disappearance of momentum returns should be a major concern.

Interestingly, this statement will apply to every strategy and factor. During the dot-com bubble, value investors had their returns pummeled, with some pundits saying they would never return to favor. Yet they did. In every cycle, things come into favor and then out of favor. When you view the data for momentum, this myth disappears swiftly. Furthermore, there is no proof of a loss in momentum as institutional investors have exhibited heightened interest, and expenses have gone down.

Mind you, from my experience, in times of flat and drifting markets, one has more difficulty securing profits. It is like a fish out of water flapping around. Also, in a quick spiking market, moves are violent from up to down or vice versa.

MYTH NO. 8: MOMENTUM IS TOO VOLATILE TO RELY ON

In times of uncertainty, everything becomes too volatile. The spring of 2009 and the beginning of COVID-19 were a time of extreme volatility. Momentum does not make money every time, but it will over time. You didn't make money with momentum strategies in 2008-2009, and you didn't make money in value strategies in 1999-2000. 1930 was bad for value investors, as 1932 was ugly for momentum investors.

Myth number 9: Various momentum measurements can yield different outcomes within a specific timeframe.

Well, ya, you don't say. I am going to ignore this one. This is true using any strategy.

MYTH NO. 10: THERE IS NO THEORY BEHIND MOMENTUM

We can categorize most theories into two buckets. One is risk-based, the other is behavioral. In behavioral theories, you can explain momentum by either an overreaction, under-reaction, or a combination of both to new flows. Here, one can say that as long as the biases and behaviors are stable, the premium received will also be stable.

The risk theory states that taking higher risks leads to superior returns. Yet, as long as risks and the taste for risk don't change, the premium will also be stable and long-term.

In conclusion, try as they might, the myth spreaders cannot measure up to the facts, and I don't care. From my experience, momentum works, and I have seen it. I will continue to preach that it works.

> ***"Don't try to buy at the bottom and sell at the top. It can't be done except by liars."*—Bernard Baruch, American Financier.**

5. Corner Stone 2 - Relative Strength.

In my mind, Relative Strength is the must-have tool in every advisor and investor's toolbox. Don't leave home without it as the American Express ads tell us. The same is true with relative strength. You absolutely need it and to use it for effective asset management and risk control.

"Academics have been studying momentum investing for the better part of two decades. As a stand-alone investment strategy, it delivers positive abnormal returns (alpha) above the market's returns, producing even better abnormal performance than either size or value styles.... Momentum's effect exists in nearly all securities, sectors, international markets, and different asset classes. It works in large-cap, mid-cap, and small-cap stocks and among value and growth stocks, too. [19]

Researchers have conducted countless studies since this report was written 25 years ago to figure out why Relative Strength works. I have read many of those papers because I also want to know.

The efficient market theorists were content to say that the additional returns resulted from the strategies taking on additional risk. Many papers disproved this point. Let's abandon that idea.

Then, the behaviorist took a swing at it. Based on the Nobel Memorial prize-winning work of Daniel Kahneman and Amos Tversky, the behaviorist put forward several reasons. One explanation was that people reacted to new information at different

[19] Moskowitz, pp. 1

rates and at different times. A trader would act differently to new information than an investor, and so on. They believed that the extra profits resulting from relative strength could be attributed to investors reacting late to a company's news announcement. Investors would discount beginning negative news and only react after a number of negative announcements.

Yet we have seen in the Challenger case investors acted quickly, both with the negative implications on Morton Thiokol and the positive, not guilty gesture of Lockheed, Martin Marietta, and Rockwell.

The root causes of momentum or relative strength continue to be debated. The evidence supported by many markets, asset classes, and time periods shows that it is not a random event. Enough said.

Olympic Team Selection

In the realm of sports, the Olympic Games stand as the grandest platform. Athletes from every corner of the world unite to champion their nations and challenge the best of the best. Among the most esteemed events in the Olympics are Track and Field, a domain encompassing a diverse array of disciplines from sprinting to throwing to jumping. But have you ever pondered over the process our nation undertakes to select its Olympic Track team?

The journey to secure a spot in our Olympic Track team is a fierce and demanding one. Athletes must meet specific qualifying standards established by the governing body of track and field in our nation at first. The governing body of track and field in our nation crafts these standards, rooted in past performances, to ensure that only the crème de la crème earn the Olympic honor. Once the athletes meet the qualifying standards, they then compete in a series of trials or championships to earn their rightful place on the Olympic team.

These trials are fiercely competitive, as athletes vie for a few spots on the team. The selection committee only chooses the top finishers in each event to represent our country at the Olympics. But beyond just meeting qualifying standards and performing well at trials, athletes must also demonstrate their dedication to their sport and their country. They must show that they will put in the hard work and sacrifice necessary to compete at the highest level. They must embody the values of fair play, integrity, and fair play.

So, why does our nation carefully and thoroughly select its Olympic Track team? It's because the Olympics serve as a mirror reflecting our nation on the global stage. The athletes who grace the Olympics aren't just representing themselves, but their comrades, their mentors, and their entire nation. They are the envoys of our nation, and as such, they must embody the values and principles we hold dear.

Selecting our Olympic Track team in a fair and transparent manner ensures that we are sending the best athletes to compete at the Olympics. It ensures that our country is competitive and succeeds globally. It also inspires the next generation of athletes to strive for excellence and pursue their dreams of competing at the Olympics. Selecting our Olympic Track team is a rigorous and competitive one. It ensures that only the best athletes represent our country at the Olympics. It also emphasizes the values of dedication, fair play, and fair play. By meticulously selecting our Olympic Track team, we are setting our athletes up for success and inspiring future generations to pursue their Olympic dreams.

Imagine if the selection process for the Olympic track and field team was utterly different. What if a group of so-called "experts" sat in a room and decided which athletes should represent our country at the Olympics? It sounds absurd, doesn't it? That's because it is. The Olympic Trials are the fairest and most effective way to select the best athletes to represent our country on the world stage. The winners of the Trials have proven themselves to be the strongest and most competitive in their respective events, and they deserve the opportunity to compete against the best athletes from around the globe.

So, what does this have to do with investing, you may ask? Well, it's simple. Just like in sports, the best way to select future winners in the stock market is to choose the current winners. Our relative strength models identify market leaders and hold on to them as long as they remain strong. By building a portfolio of these market leaders, you can increase your chances of achieving superior returns.

You deserve to have a portfolio selection process that is as rigorous and effective as the Olympic team selection process. You deserve a gold medal portfolio to help you reach your financial goals and secure your future. Don't settle for mediocre investments or outdated strategies. Choose a winning approach that can help you succeed in the market.

The Olympic Trials exemplify how selecting winners based on current performance can lead to success. By incorporating the same principle into your investment strategy, you can increase your chances of building a successful portfolio that can withstand market fluctuations and deliver consistent returns. So, aim for gold and choose a winning investment strategy to help you achieve your financial dreams.

We use the same dedication and rigor in selecting our portfolios for who is on the team and who is not. See more details in Chapters 12-15. Also, you might wish to check out https://beyondetfspro.com

Why Relative Strength?

With each passing year, global financial markets offer more and more choices to investors. More options can be offered if investors have a logical framework to analyze this broad universe of securities. We all know that the financial markets offer ample quantities of both risks and returns. Indeed, the possibility of a return exists precisely because of the inherent risk. Financial markets continue to provide the best opportunities for investors to build and preserve long-term wealth. However, an investor needs to have a **systematic investment strategy** to capitalize on the opportunities in the financial markets.

Further in the book, I will describe and show you the successful programs we put together at BAT—Brockmann Analytics & Trading using a method aptly named THE BROCKMANN METHOD. Our Relative Strength portfolios offer a systematic approach to investing. We build each of our portfolios based on the investment factor known as relative strength.

We rely on relative strength to manage portfolios because of its adaptive nature and long-term track record of success. Relative strength is simple in concept yet powerful in application. **It is simply the comparison of price performance within a universe of securities**. Analyzing securities by their relative strength provides a way to identify the leaders from the rest of the pack. We want to own those market leaders.

Relative strength also allows us to identify the laggards. Successful investing requires avoiding the losers. Relative strength is equally good at identifying long-term winners and losers. We find that relative strength analysis is not confined just to the financial markets. We find it in our daily lives, at the supermarket, and all around us.

My selection process is simple yet very robust and, more importantly, adaptive. The image below provides a brief pictorial representation of my process. We start with a selected universe of securities. We then rank each one against the other on a price-performance basis until we have a list of the strongest performers ranked to the weakest. This process not only gives us the strongest to consider but also the weakest to be avoided.

This process lends itself well to the study of different asset classes. Are bonds leading or equities? How do International Equities rank against domestic? Is Apple stronger than Google? How does Goldman Sachs rank against its peers? Should I look at the Gold or healthcare sector? Should I be in cash?

Over time, as the price changes, so does the ranking.

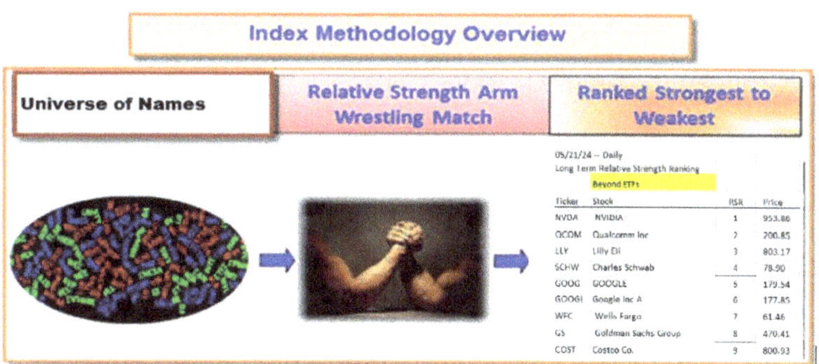

We throw out the adage of Buy Low and Sell High. Instead, we Buy High and Sell Higher. History is full of examples of securities that have faltered while analysts continued to issue buy recommendations. Investors would have sold names such as Nortel, Enron, and Research in Motion long before hitting bottom because they were underperforming and others were outpacing them.

We want to take the emotion out of the investment equation. Just what Sgt. Joe Friday would said from the old television show Dragnet... "just the facts, ma'am, just the facts." The facts show up in the price.

The graph below, courtesy of Bespoke Investment Group, tells a successful story. The chart shows two lines: one represents price, and the other represents analysts' consensus earnings estimates. There has been a dramatic drop in prices. The estimated agreement gradually decreases, but it sharply drops once earnings are reported. Now, the analysts have figured out what price knew all along. The particular example here shows an earnings miss, but the price is also often anticipatory on the upside.

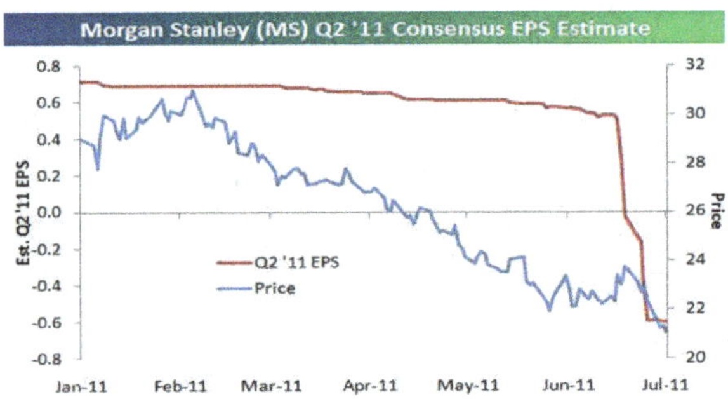

When you sort stocks by relative strength, it becomes clear that they are strong because they have superior fundamentals.

I follow the trend, up or down. I am a financial mercenary. I will change to the winning side as required.

What Moskowitz noted once again in his paper was that the time horizon of momentum is a phenomenon that exists in the 6-12-month period. Beyond 12 months, momentum wanes, and over a 3-5-year horizon, we see reversals (e.g. winners lose and losers win). However, assets that have performed well over the past 6-12 months tend to do better over the next 6-12 months than assets that have performed poorly over the same past period.

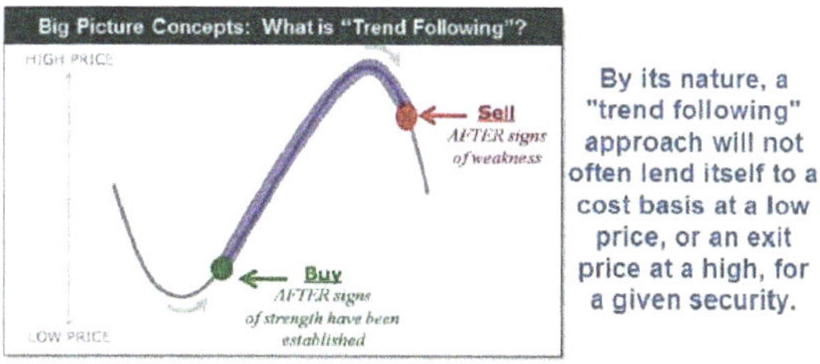

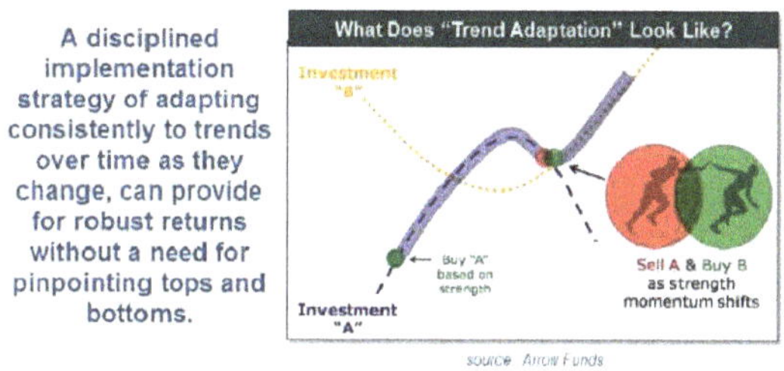

It took me some time for this reality to sink in and to move from the theoretical study phase to my trading environment. One of the first stocks I purchased under this process was a company called Constellation Software. Its trading price reached $170, representing a sharp climb from the $60 range just the year before. I have to tell you, my hands were sweaty, and my fingers hovered over the enter key. I faced a dilemma: should I press the key or not? It caused a lot of drama for me. I spent 15 minutes mustering the courage to punch the buy key as my finger hovered over it. I thought I was going to have a heart attack. I was so nervous. Here I was, buying at the top. I was going to look like a total idiot if it fell back. Once I finally hit the enter button, I had to rest another 10 minutes before repeating the whole procedure over again for another client. My nerves and heart would only allow me to enter 3 positions on that day. I left for the day to go home and recoup and to contemplate what I had just done. To go over the strategy once again.

The wonderful thing about my process is that it will tell you the two most important things every investor needs to know. What to buy and when to sell. Most people are good at the buying part of the equation but horrible at the selling part.

As I became more comfortable with this new way of doing business for myself and my clients, I became a machine. I had no emotion. I just followed the rules. I have taped the following two comments to the side of my desk so I can see them. I have a wall of comments, but these two are beside my desk.

"What's the worst thing that can happen to a quarterback?"

"He loses his confidence." Tom Bradshaw.

I am the quarterback for my clients' accounts and could not afford any missteps again, as I had during the Great Recession.

Some investors will say, for example, that they wish to have exposure to, say, the real estate or healthcare sectors. Since they don't know the best names in these areas, they will want to buy the ETF and call it a day. Or how do you pick out the winners in the technology or energy sector?

As of 21 May 2024, the SPDR Sector Technology ETF (XLK) had 65 stocks in its portfolio, and the SPDR Real Estate Sector ETF (XLRE) had 31 stocks. While the Sector Healthcare (XLV) holds 64 names. Should you choose to be exposed to these sectors, you could simply go out and buy each of the ETFs. Three tickets and you are done, BUT. Here is the rub: when you buy a basket like this, you get strong performing and underperforming names, all included. Why buy the underperformers? Remember what Warren Buffett said: you concentrate on gaining wealth and your diversity if you don't know what you are doing. Run a relative strength ranking on the list, pick out the top, and leave the laggards behind.

As Yogi Berra said, ***"In theory there is no difference between theory and practice, in practice there is."*** In this instance, diversification seems good in theory, but not so much in practice. I also discovered that the more names you add, the weaker the portfolio becomes because each new name is lower on the strength ranking list.

Letters from the Crypt

These are letters I sent out to clients 10-15 years ago. They are as relevant today as they were back then.

Trend Following Beats Market Timing

Mark Hulbert has been tracking advisory newsletters for over 20 years. Lots of these newsletters do active market timing, so in a recent column, he asked an obvious question:

The first question: How many stock market timers, of the several hundred monitored by the Hulbert Financial Digest, called the bottom of the bear market a year ago?

And a follow-up: Of those that did, how many also called the top of the bull market in March 2000 — or, for that matter, the major market turning points in October 2002 and October 2007?

If you are relying on some type of market timing to get you out of the way of bear markets and to get you into bull markets, this is exactly what you want to know. Although there are pundits who claim to have called the bottom to the day, Mr. Hulbert allowed a far more generous window for labeling a market timing call as correct... *My analysis actually relied on a far more relaxed definition: Instead of moving 100% from cash to stocks with a bottom, or 100% the other way with a top, I allowed exposure changes of just ten percentage points to qualify.*

Furthermore, rather than requiring the change in exposure to occur on the exact day of the market's top or bottom, I looked at a month-long trading window that began before the market's juncture and extended a couple of weeks thereafter.

That's a pretty liberal definition: the market timer gets a four-week window and only has to change allocations by 10% to be considered to have "called" the turn. And here's the bottom line:

Even with these relaxed criteria, however, **none of the market timers that the Hulbert Financial Digest has tracked over the last decade could call the market tops and bottoms** since March 2000.

Yep, zero. [The bold and underline is from me.] It's not that advisors aren't trying; **it's just that no one can do it successfully**, even with a one-month window and a very modest change in allocations. Obviously, there is lots of hindsight bias going on where advisors *claim* to have detected market turning points, but when Mr. Hulbert goes back to look at the actual newsletters, not one got it right! You can safely assume anyone who claims to time the market is lying. At the very least, the burden on proof is on them.

We don't bother trying to figure out what the market will do going forward. We simply follow trends as they present themselves. We use relative strength in a systematic way to identify the trends we want to follow: the strongest ones. We stay with the trend as long as it continues, whether that is for a short time or an extended period. When a trend weakens, as evidenced by its relative strength ranking, we knock that asset out of the portfolio and replace it with a stronger asset. There are many research papers that show quite clearly that it is possible to have very favorable investment results over time without any recourse to market timing at all. Discipline and patience are needed, of course, but you don't have to have a crystal ball.

—-this article originally appeared. 3/17/2010 (resent 30 May 2014) It is especially apropos now that many market pundits are busy predicting a top. It's certainly possible they are right, but the proposition that they are just guessing is probably equally likely. Over the long run there is weak evidence that market timing is effective.

Bank of England Endorses Trend Following![20]
(Which is what we do)

I confess to drastically overstating the case to get your attention. But Andrew Haldane is an economist at the Bank of England. He recently gave a speech on Patience and Finance, which was commented on by Gavyn Davies in the Financial Times. Mr.

[20] Systematic Relative Strength, The Official Blog of Dorsey Wright Money Management also Dorsey Wright & Associates Daily Equity Report for Monday, September 20, 2010

Haldane made some comments about the puzzling success of trend-following strategies versus using value, summarized by Mr. Davies:

Andy Haldane conducts the following experiment. He estimates the results of an investment strategy in US equities, which is based entirely on the past direction of the stock market. If the market rises in the period just ended, the strategy buys stocks for the next period, and vice versa. The strategy simply extrapolates the recent trend in the market. The result? According to Andy, if you had been wise enough to start this procedure with $1 in 1880, you would have consistently shifted in and out of stocks at the right times, and you would now possess over $50,000. Not bad for a strategy which could have been designed in a kindergarten.

Next, Andy tries an alternative strategy based on value. This calculates whether the stock market is overvalued or undervalued and buys the market only when the value gives a positive signal. The criterion for measuring value is the dividend discount model, first devised by Robert Shiller. If you had been clever enough to devise this measure of value investing in 1880 and had invested $1, the procedure would have left you with a portfolio now worth the princely sum of 11 cents.

I am sure that fundamentalists will argue that this value strategy is far too simple and that other ways of using the Shiller p/e or alternative measures of value would produce much better results. That may be the case, but it does not detract from the fact that a very basic momentum-based technique seems to work very well indeed. And that should not be true if you believe in the efficiency of capital markets.

I'm not too surprised by the good performance of the trend-following strategy (but I am shocked by the terrible, terrible performance of the dividend discount model). Clearly, the momentum factor captures some universal characteristics. Maybe it is something psychological like investor confidence, or perhaps it is closely related to the underlying fundamentals and the business cycle.

As Mr. Davies points out, this observation is very problematic for efficient markets and Modern Portfolio Theory. The whole rise of passive investing–using index funds and giving up on picking stocks–is based on the assumption that markets are efficient. I see this indexing approach extolled for individual investors all the time now. However, if markets are not efficient, for whatever reason, passive investing is bunk.

I have to come down on the bunk side of the ledger. The momentum anomaly is far too well-established for claims that passive investing is the only thing that makes sense. Whatever the underlying process is, it has worked since 1880–and continues to work today. (Some of our published research shows that models written about almost 40 years ago still generate a similar level of excess return in today's markets, so it's not simply a case of the anomaly being unknown.)

Instead, why not take advantage of relative strength as a return factor? Maybe the trend followed by relative strength is finally coming into its own.

Sincerely

6. The First Principal.

"Prices are never too high to begin buying and never too low to begin selling."

- Jesse Livermore

"Buy high and sell higher."

The adage "Buy low and sell High" may be mistaken. I have since learned it should be "Buy high and sell higher." This pearl of wisdom came from researching the life and history of Jesse Livermore, the world's greatest stock trader.

Jesse Livermore was indeed the world's greatest stock trader. He believed the market was a study in cycles, as in life. The new trend will continue until the momentum weakens. Like, Sir. Isaac Newton stated, "A body in motion tends to stay in motion until it means an equal or greater force." Livermore was a trader who was only interested in price and trend. He viewed investing in stocks as trading a piece of paper based on the behavior of other market participants.

I have never understood why people place special attributes on securities as if they differ from any other asset one might own. If I buy a car that is a lemon, I will not hold on to it in the hopes it will improve. I'd replace it and move on. Yet people feel they have to break even on a trade before moving on. No, if it meets a sell criteria, sell it. Chapter 14 will cover additional information about my buying and selling requirements.

Livermore was incredibly unique and significantly ahead of his time. Throughout his life, he was always learning and adapting. He always considered himself a market student who occasionally traded correctly. [21] What makes a good stock speculator, you ask? He would say you would need the aptitude for the game, a stomach for the ride, and to see what is happening without emotion. [22]

In a discussion while at Palm Beach, he reportedly stated, "Don't take tips of any kind, no matter where they come from." *Don't worry about catching the top or bottoms, that's fool's play. Keep the number of stock you own to a controllable number. It's hard to herd cats, and it's hard to track a lot of securities. Take your losses quickly and don't brood about them. Try to learn from them..... Finally, like the markets, you gotta do and love math. So while others are talking and talking and talking, like they always do, you can be thinking and thinking and thinking, figuring the percentages and the probabilities.* [23]

Once I exit a position, I remove it from my monitors. I don't care about the stock once I am out of it. It is easily forgotten when it is not in view. When a security needs to go, it goes. If it performs well again, it comes back in. It has no good or bad memories. They are just numbers.

Livermore's rules are often based on thinking and acting against the grain: [24]

[21] Smitten, pp.128
[22] Smitten, pp.128. Livermore in discussion with Bradley's Beach Club in Palm Beach.
[23] Smitten, pp. 130-132. Continuation of the discussion at the Beach Club.
[24] Smitten, R., 2001, 'Jesse LIVERMORE World's Greatest Stock Trader, John Wiley & Sons, New York

- ✓ Cut your losses promptly.
- ✓ Be sure to confirm your judgment before you take your full position.
- ✓ Let your profits ride if there is no reason to close out the position.
- ✓ The action is with the leading stocks, which change with every new market.
- ✓ Keep the number of stocks you follow limited in order to focus.
- ✓ New all-time highs are to be bought on breakouts.
- ✓ Cheap stocks often appear to be bargains after a large drop. They often continue to fall or have little potential to rise in price. Leave them alone!
- ✓ Use pivotal points to identify changes in trends and confirmations of trends.
- ✓ Don't fight the tape!
- ✓ Smile; that is my rule.

Rule are Rules

Yes, Rules are Rules, and they are meant to be followed. There are several reasons why we choose to follow them. First, it takes the guesswork out of making decisions. Admittedly, it's emotionally lazy, but let me tell you, it's absolutely worth it. You aspire to be like a robot or a cyborg. You come across a situation and know how to deal with it. If A, then you do B. End of story. No second guessing. No, should I wait a little longer? There is no emotion. Go and do the crossword puzzles, then. It reduces stress and safeguards your emotional reserves, your emotional capital.

You have two types of capital: the capital in your account and the emotional capital. Sometimes, the emotional capital is more important than the funds in your account. How often have I had to stop myself from worrying about a position? I have a quote from Glenn Turner taped just above my monitors: "Worrying is like a rocking chair. It gives you something to do, but it doesn't get you anywhere." So, stop worrying. See how easy that is?

How true that is in markets and in your own life as well.

It's Okay to Be Wrong, But Never Okay to Stay Wrong

I have many examples of trends that were captured beautifully, but just as many that don't turn out so well. It's fine as long as we abandon unsuccessful trends before they become disastrous. Trend-following portfolios won't always provide excess returns, but if you're far more concerned about "over time" than "every time," there is a place for these strategies in your portfolio.

I have always felt that a successful trade is one in which you **hate yourself for selling before you hate yourself for not selling.** If you are in a losing trade, close it out, shake the dust from your shoes, and move on. They say your last breath is important, but not as important as your next breath. The same goes for trading.

Beyond ETFs Pro

		Winners	Losers
Start date:	01/02/07		
End date:	06/30/24		
Number of trades:	493	245	248
Average periods per trade:	119.46	175.64	63.96
Maximum Profit/Loss:		468.70 %	(38.22)%
Average Drawdown:	(5.91)%	(3.32)%	(8.46)%
Average Profit/Loss:	8.05 %	22.54 %	(6.27)%
Probability:		49.70 %	50.30 %
Average Annual ROI:	24.59 %	46.85 %	(35.80)%
Reward/Risk Ratio:	3.55		
Portfolio:			
Starting Balance:	100000.00		
Ending Balance:	2510844.62		
Gain/Loss:	2410844.62		
Gain/Loss (IRR) %:	2410.84 %	Annualized:	20.21 %
Drawdown:		From	To
Maximum Continuous:	(15.16)%	06/07/22	06/17/22
Portfolio High:	(4.44)%	06/18/24	06/24/24
Peak/Valley:	(30.47)%	02/19/20	03/23/20

In the portfolio used in the Beyond ETFs Pro app, there have been 245 winning trades, 248 losing trades. There have been more losers than winners, yet the return generated from 2 January 2007 to 30 June 2024 has been 20.21% annualized. The average hold period for the winning trades was 175.64 days, while the loser's average hold period was 63.96 days.

So, the model generated a return of 20.21% annually to the S&P 100 index of 8.25%.

You can see that our trading rules capture the understanding that Livermore came to understand. We cut losses quickly and let our profits run. For current, up-to-date results, you can view them at https://beyondetfspro.com in the “our numbers” section.

Once you grasp and understand the concept and implications of momentum, things fall into place. We use many of the concepts of momentum in our daily lives. For example, if I were to ask you who you think will be in the top 10 ranking of the PGA next year, you would most likely look at this year's top 10 and pick from that list. Someone might jump from nowhere to claim one of those spots, but it is highly unlikely. Speaking of golf, I am sending a shout-out to my two nieces, who one day will be in the top 10 of the LPGA, Maddie and Ellie Szeryk. They are not there yet, but they have the momentum building behind them.

The same is true with momentum in stocks. There is a high probability that the leadership today will be the leadership tomorrow until the momentum changes and someone takes over those spots. I return to the Moskowitz paper; stocks performing strongly in the last 6-12 months will most likely continue to perform well for the next 6-12 months. Securities that have been performing poorly for the last 6-12 months will continue to perform poorly for the next 6-12 months. Livermore's rules are all about momentum. Cut your losses quickly, he says, because the momentum is not with you. Let your profits ride if there is no reason to sell. Again, here, the market will tell you when to get out. When he speaks about buying the breakout of stocks that have reached their 52-week high, it is because the momentum is strong.

I find it interesting when he discusses maintaining a small, manageable list of securities. Even Warren Buffet believes in maintaining a small, manageable list of securities. Buffet said, *'You concentrate to gain wealth; you diversify if you don't know what you are doing."* Here we are not talking about one or two positions and then again, not 50-100 positions.

"*Perhaps the best-known investment paradigm is buy low, sell high. I believe that more money can be made buying high and selling at even higher prices. I try to buy stocks that have already had good price moves, that are often making new highs and that have positive relative strength. These are stocks that are in demand by other investors. What is the risk? Obviously, the risk is that I'm buying near the top. But, I would much rather be invested in a stock that is increasing in price and take the risk that it may begin to decline than invest in a stock that is already in decline and try to guess when it will turn around."* - Richard Driehaus — Driehaus Capital Management

In 2000, Barron included him in their "All-Century" team, which featured 25 individuals who had greatly influenced the mutual fund industry over the past 100 years. I remember meeting and listening to him give a presentation in the 80s. He was outstanding and one of the first managers to get me thinking about this money management style. Driehaus had an astonishingly quick response when getting out of positions. I laugh when I think back about it. It seemed his idea of long-term was to hold to the next day. The turn rate was very high, yet he was very profitable.

So, we throw out the adage of Buy Low and Sell High. Instead, we Buy High and Sell Higher. As I have mentioned, history is full of examples of securities that have faltered while analysts continue issuing buy recommendations. They cling to their convictions, attempting to will the market to their point of view. For me, value investors take the same stance.

I am reminded of a story concerning one of the firm's analysts. A client asked me what I thought of this one particular stock. I was unfamiliar with it, so I put it on my A list to see how it ranked against others in the universe. It had an acceptable ranking, but it didn't excel like others did. I told him I would watch it, and if it moved up in the rankings, we would add it to his portfolio. Over a couple of months, it rose, and we added it to his portfolio when it reached the $18 range. It continued to rank well, and the price peaked at around $31-32. It started to drift lower, and at $28.50, it gave a sell signal, so we sold it. Selling it left the client feeling disappointed, as he had extensively researched and firmly believed in its value and potential. Yes, it dominated a new industry category, but it was losing ground in the rankings. I explained to him that it had dropped and that other positions showed stronger potential at that moment. It hit our sell signal, and when the stock performed and ranked better, we would buy it back. Currently, it was in the zone for selling.

As stated, I disregarded the firm's research publication because of its irrelevance to my investing style and lack of significance. I would go around to the rookies, handing out the hard copies that would land on my desk. I have to laugh about this one memory. While getting a coffee, a group of rookies had gathered and talked among themselves, so I joined in. As the discussion progressed, one told me management had instructed them not to talk to me. I laughed and laughed.

Each morning, there was a publication that summarized in a few words what the analysis was thinking about their particular stocks. This one morning, what caught my eye was not only the mention of the stock we had sold but also the message was in upper caps. I read that the analysis was pounding the table to buy this stock today because they would report earnings tomorrow and beat the-street estimates.

The report's aggressive nature left me in shock. It caused me a moment of self-doubt and forced me to review my analysis of the stock again, re-check the rankings and look again at the chart. I reflected for a few minutes and stood my ground. The analyst was wrong, I felt. The earnings might be good, but the stock wasn't a buy. I was so confident in my stance that I sent the enlarged and more in-depth report to the client, saying that the analyst was mistaken and that we would watch it and not buy any. I was just so cocky. You may strive to be humble, but sometimes, it's difficult to remain that way.

So, I waited the next morning for the earnings announcement. It had closed at $23.25 the previous night. I have to tell you I was a little nervous. OK, I was a lot nervous. Why was I so cocky and so arrogant to send the report to the client to taunt the analyst's prediction?

The earning announcement came before the market opened, and it was beat on the street estimates—a big beat. My heart sank… until the market opened. The first trade was $18.75. I was relieved and never did that again.

My process is right over time, not every time.

GTAT

In mid-2013, GT Advanced Technologies (GTAT) caught my attention, so I added it to my "A" watch list. I pay attention to several watch lists. I have my A list and a few B and C lists. I treat them like I am running a baseball franchise. If a stock shows promise, I sign it to the minor leagues. If they keep improving, they might get a call to the "show." GTAT gets the call-up and is elevated to player status to be placed into the portfolio buy camp. (I will explain and go through my buy and sell discipline later in the book.)

I bought the stock for several clients. It rose in rankings and price but underperformed in the fall of that year. It went sideways for a while and then met my sell conditions, so I sold it. For me, a stock could get a sell signal even if it continues to rise or go sideways. Here, other stocks were rising faster than GTAT.

It began performing better in January 2014, and I added it back to my buy list, so I purchased it for around $8 in January and continued buying through April. It peaked at $19-ish in April and then drifted lower. I took some profits in May at the $17 range, and then it nosedived to $14.76. I looked at the rankings, and it gave me a sell signal, so I immediately called the remaining clients, and we sold that day.

Management and compliance were on me like a duck on a June bug. They demanded to see my reasons for the quick turnaround. They felt I was churning the accounts and wanted to hold me to account. Churning is when the broker buys and sells to generate commissions to the benefit of the broker and not the client. They said I was foolish and an idiot (their words) because GTAT had secured a $500 million loan from Apple. GTAT provided Apple with the glass covers for their iPhones.

Management demanded to know how successful the accounts were. I elaborated to them that a successful trade involved adhering to my process, regardless of the outcome.

I gathered the requested information and showed on the charts that the stock had fallen and had given me a sell signal. Of the 23 positions I sold that day, 21 were profitable, with the smallest profit being +34%, the highest profit being +84%, and two losses of -12% and -18 %. I stood my ground, yet I began to think that I might have overreacted for a few months that summer, **until GTAT filed for bankruptcy on October 6, 2014.**

Did I have inside information? No. Did the analysts get it wrong? Yes. I had the same information every investor had at my disposal—the price action. It didn't matter what the company said, what the analyst said, or what my management said.

The price action wasn't satisfactory even with a large and stable financier and customers like Apple backing them up. Here, the wisdom of the crowd saw this company for what it was: a stock in decline. And so did I. To be honest, the bankruptcy shook me. I thought at first that maybe an angel had come and tapped me on the shoulder that day, but after reviewing my records, I did get a sell signal and followed up on it.

I wish I had this knowledge years back and used it with Nortel, Blackberry, Enron, and countless other names that disappointed and fell from great heights.

Painting the Tape

I want to share a story from my past that I thought, in hindsight, is amusing now. Back in the olden days, which felt like yesterday, we didn't have access to the technology we do today. Technology has greatly democratized investing. Costs of everything related to the financial services industry have been driven downward and continue to be so today. Remember, we could only rely on the Dow Jones News Wire and our squeak boxes, which allowed managers and analysts to broadcast from headquarters and printed newspapers to access information.

So here is the scene: It is the early 1980s at the Merrill Lynch Canada London Ontario office. We, brokers, are organized in pairs, with the newest ones positioned upfront near the ticker tape, and the more experienced brokers further back. The commodity brokers are at the very back. The bullpen environment allowed for no privacy, and you shared a quote machine with your desk partner.

Dale, the receptionist, calls out, *"Call in, line 1. Call in, line 2."* My desk partner, John, who sat to my right and was on call-ins that day, looked up at me. He takes line 1, and then I take line 2. My caller was a gentleman with a thick Scottish accent who said to me he wanted to buy $100,000 of Dome Petroleum; what did he need to do? I told him he needed to come into the office, open an account, and write the cheque in front of me. I gave him my name and direct number, and he said he'll be there next week. The call didn't last long, and when I finished, I looked over at John, and he asked me what I got. I told him someone is asking for a quote on Dome; he said someone was asking for a quote on Bell. We go about our day and think nothing of the call.

A week later, the gentlemen showed up at the office, to my surprise and delight. We chatted about his background in the oil industry, how he has worked worldwide in various countries and environments, and that he loves Dome Petroleum. We opened the account, he wrote the cheque, and I told him about the wonders of margin. With a margin account, we can buy even more of Dome. He agrees, and he departs. I am waiting for the account to be opened.

Sometime later, the account is approved and opened. I call the client to confirm the order. "*Buy XXX shares of Dome Petroleum at market.*" I sprinted to the security cage, timestamped the order, returned to my desk, and waited for the fill.

As I sit down, Mark W yells out, "*There's a takeover on Dome!!*" We all jump up and run over and crowd around the Dow Wire. Someone is pulling back the rolled up tape frantically, looking for any hints of news. I am now in the second row, trying to look over the shoulders of my colleagues to see the wire as well. I mutter, I am sure lucky I just bought Dome. Someone turns to me and asks how much, so I tell him. Everyone stops, turns, and stares at me. *"You idiot, you are supposed to go through the block desk so you don't disrupt the markets.* With that, everyone gloomily went back to their desk. The excitement was over this time, and I am a little wiser.

When reading the ticker tape, you look for patterns. What is the size of the trades? Which symbol is being traded? Are companies in the same industry being traded alongside each other? Are the trades on upticks, or is the stock moving lower? What we saw with my Dome trade was only Dome moving across the tape. There were no other trades being reported—only Dome. ***I painted the tape***. More reading the tape stories later.

Here is a client letter sent out in March 2014. It describes how someone should pick the annual March Madness college basketball tournament brackets. It also tells us how we should look at our investment portfolio.

Dear:

This is a wonderful time of year for anyone who follows college basketball. That's because the NCAA Division I Men's and Women's Basketball Tournaments are underway in a run of games spanning a two-and-a-half week period that is euphemistically referred to as March Madness.

That moniker is among the best in sports because crazy things do indeed happen when these tournaments begin. There are buzzer beaters; there are upsets (otherwise known as bracket busters); there is total domination; and there is almost always at least one team that carries the Cinderella banner past the first two rounds into the Sweet 16.

The *Wall Street J*ournal on March 18, 2014, had an article on how to win your NCAA Office Pool:

"Pick the favorites. This is the only foolproof way to guarantee you won't embarrass yourself. For all of the attention paid to underdogs—is there any other reason you know Florida Gulf Coast University exists?—the better team still wins most round-of-64 games. Over the last 10 seasons, the average number of double-digit seeds beating favorites was six per tournament. Meanwhile, a company spokeswoman said that a bracket with favorites winning

every game last year would have placed in the 91st percentile of entries to ESPN's contest. Your bracket can only be so contrary until it's cuckoo".

Part of the fun of NCAA Office Pools is bragging rights of picking the underdogs (even if it's a statistical unlikelihood). However, this same principle applies to investing. When it comes to the financial markets, **rather than shoot for bragging rights, go for the money!**

Something else that stands out about the tournaments is that many of the same basketball programs are regarded as national championship contenders year after year. These are blue chip programs. There are other schools in that blue chip mix as well. The point is that the blue chip label has been earned from a longstanding history of competitive success that has earned the program national recognition, a large fan base, and the respect of its opponents. It is said that success breeds success. That rings true in college basketball as it does in following an investment approach.

Nobody's Perfect

March Madness isn't just limited to the NCAA tournaments. There has been a little March madness this year as well in the stock market, the global economy, the geopolitical arena, and the weather.

That madness has created some volatility, some speculative excess in certain situations, some misgivings about growth prospects, and a whole lot of calls for the head of Punxsutawney Phil and Wharton Willy.

It is precisely at maddening times like these that investors should have a renewed appreciation for a disciplined process and approach. The fine investment strategy I use, which employs relative strength, isn't perfect. It experiences operational disappointments now and then, and its performance suffers as a result.

Even Duke, which has one of the most respected programs in men's college basketball, hasn't made the NCAA Tournament every year. It missed the NCAA Tournament in 1995, but it has been back every year since. Only Duke fans (and probably North Carolina fans) can recall that 1995 blemish. What the rest of the college basketball world knows and respects is that Duke has made 37 tournament appearances, 15 Final Four appearances, and has won four national championships.

Reputation Precedes Itself

It's no mystery why Duke, in most years, is picked in NCAA brackets as a team expected to go a long way in the tournament. Duke, of course, has been a bracket bust before, which is akin to a blue chip company having a one-time earnings disappointment. The overriding point is that Duke's longstanding history of success makes it a safe selection more often than not to produce some nice bracket returns.

It isn't really all that different for investment approaches as well. They are expected to do well year after year. They stumble occasionally, but quality management, discipline, a continued desire to get better in their practices, and an adherence to a business model that has served them reliably for decades usually help them get things turned around relatively quickly and produce nice returns for investors

When filling out a tournament bracket, it is easy to overthink things because there is so much noise in the echo chamber. There is no shortage of opinions about which teams will do well and which won't. Expert cheat sheets are published on sports sites and they get parsed in an attempt to predict the first round upsets and to identify Cinderella. This happens because crazy things happen in the early rounds, and calling those early upsets can be the difference in winning an office pool.

When it comes to winning the whole thing, though, Cinderella is not the safe bet. The blue chip programs are the safe bet and there is plenty of tournament history to back that up.

The same process of overthinking things happens just as readily in the stock market.

Innumerable opinions are put forth about which stocks will do well and which won't. That is why I use relative strength. It has a proven track record of success. It is not right every time but over time.

Again, when it comes to the financial markets, **rather than shoot for bragging rights, go for the money!** We select from the options that are there, not from the options that used to be there, and especially not from the options that we think "should be" there in a moral sense. That is why we use our relative strength processes in our models and go for the money.

Sincerely

Wilf

----

7. The Second Principal

"When the facts change, I change my mind. What do you do, Sir? – John M Keynes

I came across the following note I sent to clients over 20 years ago. It remains just as relevant now as it did back then. It describes my second plank well: changing your mind or direction when needed. Recall the observations in Tetlock's research paper and Dan Gardner's interviews, which suggest that the more famous you are, the less likely you are to change your mind. You see, we wish and need to be financial mercenaries. We want to fight on the winning side, whatever that may be. Our loyalty lies with you and your bottom line, not with some abstract idea. People have frequently asked me over the years why I don't invest in companies in my backyard. Why am I so unpatriotic? I explain that I may invest over there but spend the profits here.

As I mentioned before, when a security needs to go, it goes. If it performs well again, it comes back in. It has no good or bad memories—they are just numbers. Changing directions or course of action is challenging for many people. People don't like to admit they might have made a mistake. Take responsibility for any mistakes and keep moving forward.

Aug 8/10

When the facts change, I change my mind. What do you do, sir? ----John Maynard Keynes

Although their theories seem to be no more or no less accurate, British economists always seem to have better quips than other economists. Keynes brings up an important point. What do you do when the facts change -- and how do you know if the facts have changed?

CSS Analytics has an interesting post on this subject on Aug 5, 2010. The author points out a problem with forecasting:

The strangest thing about the forecasting world is not that it is a dismal science (which it is) but that forecasters share some remarkably primitive biases. Whether you look at purely quantitative forecasts or "expert/guru" forecasts, they have one thing in common: ***they rarely change their opinions or methods in light of new information****. In fact, what I have noticed is that the smarter the person is and the more information they seem to possess, the less likely they are to change their mind. Undoubtedly, this is why many genuinely intelligent and knowledgeable experts have blown up large funds or personal trading accounts.*

It wouldn't be so sad if it weren't true. This lack of adaptability wiped out even a couple of Nobel Prize winners at Long Term Capital Management. The problem really is one of properly structuring one's decision framework. CSS Analytics observes:

Ask a person to give you an opinion on where a market is going, and then notice what happens when the market goes dramatically the other way, along with news announcements that seem to conflict with their thesis. Most of the time, this person will tell you that they have not changed their mind, and in fact that it is an even better price to buy (or short). Models or systems suffer from the same problem–they rarely adjust as conditions or regimes change...

Here, the decision framework is fixed. Since humans are naturally wired to seek out confirming evidence and ignore disconfirming evidence, that is exactly what happens. All evidence begins to be massaged to support the opinion, which is assumed to be correct. The story from CSS Analytics below is sadly familiar to most investors, almost all of whom start out as value investors:

I spent my early investing experiences as a "value investor," and let me tell you that I learned the hard way many times that the market was more often right than wrong. It was uncanny how well future fundamentals were sometimes "forecasted" by price. I had no knowledge of technical analysis and lacked the intellectual framework to synthesize a superior decision-making method. Of course, I would ride that "undervalued" stock with a price-to-book ratio of less than 1 all the way to being a penny stock before I gave up. I also sold many of my winners far too early because their P/E ratios indicated they were no longer undervalued. Some of these stocks went on to rise by 400% or more, while I was content to make a 25% profit. I did the exact opposite with overvalued stocks or stocks with poor fundamentals. I was heavily short on Fannie Mae, Freddie Mac, and General Motors in early 2007! Of course, I got my clock cleaned and received margin calls long before they plunged almost to zero. This was a case of being right but too early to fight the sentiment of the crowd..

As a wise man once said, **"Being early is indistinguishable from being wrong."** Even knowing that we should avoid a fixed decision framework, however, doesn't really get us any closer to knowing how to handle the forecasting problem. CSS Analytics describes their epiphany:

It finally dawned on me one day that good forecasting (or decision-making) was a dynamic process involving feedback. In fact, the actual information used to make the initial decisions need not be complex as long as you are willing to adjust after the fact.

I put the whole thing in bold because I think it's that important -- although I don't think my systematic relative strength process is forecasting at all. It's simply a decision-making framework that incorporates a specific kind of feedback: the most important feedback to an investor, which is price. Price change tells you whether your decision is working out or not. If something isn't working, you kick it out of the portfolio--that's adjusting after the fact. Price is not complex at all, but it is the one-critical piece of feedback that is needed because that's how every investment is measured.

Investing is one of those weird fields where clever opinions are often more valued than results. Certain gurus still get media exposure and sell hordes of newsletter subscriptions because subscribers agree with their bullish or bearish opinions, even though an outside service like Hulbert can demonstrate that their actual performance is abysmal. In professional sports, if you suck, you get released or sit on the bench. If you really suck, you don't make the roster. Sometimes, in the investment field, if you really suck, you get to be on CNBC and have well-coiffed, polite hosts who take your opinions seriously.

I think the description of good decision-making as a dynamic process involving feedback is very concise. **Incorporating feedback is what makes a model adaptive**. Models that are based on historical data range blow up all the time for this very reason--they are optimized to the historical data but cannot always incorporate feedback. Continuous measurement of relative strength is not unlike former New York City mayor Ed Koch's greeting, "How am I doing?" If the answer is "not well," then it's time to ditch that asset and replace it with another one that has the prospect of better performance. The beauty of the relative strength models which I use is that when the facts change, it changes its mind.

Enjoy the afternoon

Wilf

Long-Term Capital Management

Many people have forgotten the tale of Long Term Capital Management, a cautionary story of the hubris leading to the eventual downfall of one of history's most renowned hedge funds. Founded in 1994 by former Salomon Brothers bond trader John Meriwether, Long Term Capital Management (LTCM) rapidly rose to prominence because of its impressive returns and a star-studded roster of investors and board members.

At its peak, LTCM managed over $100 billion in assets and was considered one of the most successful hedge funds in the world. LTCM counted two Nobel laureates, Myron Scholes and Robert C. Merton, who shared the Nobel Prize in Economics in 1997 for their work on the Black–Scholes model as part of their talent pool. They were part of the board of directors and provided the theoretical foundation for the fund's trading strategies. The fund quickly gained a reputation for its sophisticated mathematical models and talented team of traders, which included former academics and professionals from top Wall Street firms.

The financial deregulation of the late 20th century, which allowed for the creation of complex financial instruments such as derivatives, traces back to the historical context of LTCM's rise to fame. These instruments provided the perfect playground for LTCM's highly quantitative trading strategies, which were based on mathematical models that attempted to accurately predict market movements. Warren Buffett called derivatives "*Financial weapons of mass destruction.*"

Under Meriwether's leadership, LTCM grew and amassed billions of dollars in assets under management. The fund's success attracted some of the biggest names in finance, including banks, pension funds, and wealthy individuals who were eager to invest in what seemed like a sure bet. Investors and banks became enchanted and enamored with management, allowing significantly higher leverage ratios than for us mere mortals.

LTCM's undoing came when the Asian financial crisis of 1997 and the Russian debt default of 1998 sent shockwaves through the global financial markets. The fund, which had pursued even greater returns by taking on massive leverage, found itself on the wrong side of these events and suffered catastrophic losses. Rather than downsizing their positions, they continued to increase their bets. They did not heed my second pillar: "*when the facts change my mind when the facts change. What do you do, Sir?*"

Despite the intervention of the Federal Reserve and a consortium of Wall Street banks, LTCM eventually had to liquidate its positions and shut down. The fund's collapse had far-reaching consequences, triggering a liquidity crisis in the financial markets and exposing the dangers of excessive risk-taking in pursuing short-term profits. This is a fact that many people have forgotten.

LTCM's aggressive investment strategies, aimed at exploiting pricing discrepancies in global markets, eventually led to its spectacular collapse in 1998. This event, often overlooked, was a lead-up to the 2008-2009 Great Recession. LTCM stands as a stark cautionary tale, highlighting the risks associated with excessive leverage, the interconnectedness of financial markets, and the unwillingness to alter one's stance.

The LTCM debacle had an impact not only in the financial world but also in the academic community, where economists and scholars debated the implications of the fund's failure for the broader economy. Some claimed that LTCM's downfall was a unique event with no systemic risk, while others cautioned about the possibility of recurrence without learning from history.

Cue the subprime disaster.

Despite its initial success and impressive roster of talent, LTCM's downfall resulted from flawed risk management, excessive leverage, and a failure to adapt to the changing environment and news flow. They failed to note my second and third principal.

[25]I stumbled across Ed Borgato while wandering around on X (Formerly Twitter) and liked his comments. They are insightful and pertinent to investing, the markets, and life.

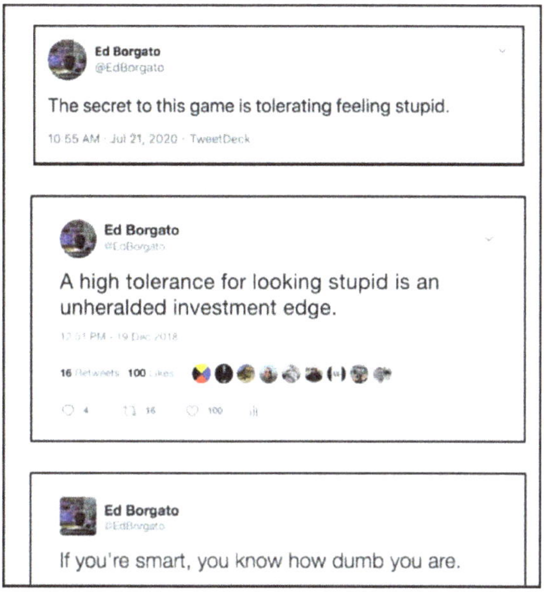

These three are particularly important to highlight. When one is grappling with deciding, it takes courage to pull the trigger and storm ahead. Yet, when one discovers that the facts that led to the decision have changed, it takes even more courage and, importantly, humility to correct them. Don't second-guess yourself. You will only waste your time and energy.

Before making it, you should have already determined the factors that would make you change your mind. If A happens, then my course of action is B. Next. Move on. Afterwards, you can evaluate your decision-making to uncover any overlooked factors.

I have found that humble pie keeps you focused and down to earth.

[25] Borgato, E, X (Formerly known as Twitter), 19 Dec 2017 & 21 Jul 2020

8. The Third Principal –

"A man should look for what is, and not for what he thinks should be."

- Albert Einstein

Albert Einstein's famous quote not only holds wisdom for life but also unintentionally provides valuable investment advice. This quote encapsulates the essence of rational decision-making and the importance of basing investment choices on reality rather than speculation. It holds significant relevance because it emphasizes the importance of rationality and objectivity in decision-making, urging individuals to focus on reality rather than their own subjective beliefs or wishes. In the realm of investing, this principle is crucial for making informed and strategic decisions that maximize returns and mitigate risks.

The importance here is to focus on your plan, which needs to be rules-based with a track record of success. This is one thing we can provide for you. I see myself as a financial zealot seeking the best for you and my clients. I am a financial cyborg who follows the rules of engagement as dispassionately as a surgeon's scalp cutting through tissue. If the rules say buy, we buy. If we sell, we sell. There's no room for second guessing. There are no thoughts, only actions.

This pillar is the most difficult of the three to implement. It's about being in the now, not in the past or future, but right now—being in the present. This is the same stance one must take to meditate. You become simple and let everything go. I have told many people that praying is good at saving the soul, but it is not so good at saving your portfolio. Believe me, I have done my share of praying.

The world of finance and investment is rife with speculation, and many individuals are driven by emotions, biases, and wishful thinking when making investment decisions. Dreaming does not make for good financial results. Successful investing requires a rational and objective approach, focusing on facts, data, and analysis rather than unfounded beliefs, tips, or hopes. By focusing on what is, investors can assess market conditions, analyze financial data, and make well-informed choices that are grounded in reality. This approach helps to minimize the impact of emotions, biases, and irrational behavior that can lead to poor investment decisions.

There are countless examples of investors who have fallen into the trap of speculation and wishful thinking, ignoring the reality of market conditions and making risky bets based on unfounded beliefs. The dot-com bubble of the late 1990s and the subprime mortgage crisis of 2008 are stark reminders of the dangers of ignoring what is in favor of what one thinks should be.

Sir Isaac Newton, the esteemed scientist, got caught up in one of the world's first investment "bubbles" related to the stock market. During the South Sea Company bubble in 1720, when the company's shares skyrocketed and then crashed, Newton's investments evaporated. Frustrated by the market's irrational behavior, he reportedly said, "*I can calculate the motions of the heavenly bodies, but not the madness of the people.*"[26] It's a reminder that market dynamics, just as in Long Term Capital Management's case, can baffle even brilliant minds.

[26] Eschner, K, 'The Market Crash That Cost Newton a Fortune, 6 Jan, 2017, Smithsonian Magazine

As technology advances and new opportunities and risks emerge, it will be essential for investors to maintain a clear-headed and objective approach, focusing on what is real and tangible rather than succumbing to the allure of speculation.

In this context, exploring the various perspectives and conducting a well-reasoned analysis is important. On the positive side, adopting a realistic and objective approach to investing can lead to better outcomes, increased portfolio performance, and greater resilience in the face of market volatility. Investors can make more informed decisions, identify opportunities, and manage risks by focusing on what is. Balancing a commitment to reality with a willingness to explore new possibilities is key to achieving success in investing. This is where BAT – Brockmann Analytics & Trading can assist you in achieving your goals at https://beyondetfspro.com

Investors who embrace the principles embedded in Einstein's quote can navigate the complexities of the market with greater confidence, adaptability, and resilience. By seeking what is rather than what they think should be, investors can make informed decisions, capitalize on opportunities, and navigate challenges effectively. By following this philosophy, investors can increase their chances of success and navigate the turbulent waters of the financial markets with confidence and clarity.

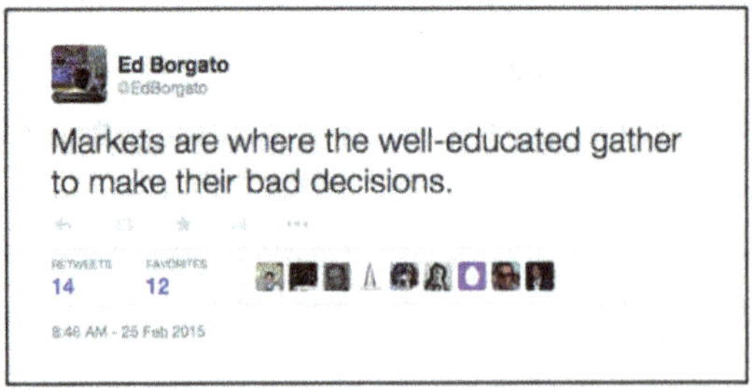

Here is another comment from Ed Borgato. It is true because we all perceive ourselves as smart, intelligent, and attractive. We do all the work to come up with an action plan, and then circumstances

change. We might have been so bold as to actually tell someone our plan. Now, have we made a change? Have we invested all this emotional capital in this trade all for nothing?

9. Foundational Principals – to live by and invest by

I abide by those principles. They are straightforward and are the tapestry woven into the foundation of my investment process.

1. "Prices are never too high to begin buying and never too low to begin selling." - Jess Livermore

2. "When the facts change, I change my mind. What do you do, sir?" - John Maynard Keynes

3. "A man should look for what is, and not for what he thinks should be" - Albert Einstein

These principles offer valuable guidance to investors, emphasizing the importance of staying flexible, being objective, and focusing on reality rather than speculation. Each principle has its own unique perspective and significance, contributing to the overall understanding and practice of investment strategies.

Jess Livermore, a legendary stock trader from the early 20th century, gained renown for his bold and unconventional approach to investing. Livermore's principle suggests market sentiment or conventional wisdom should not influence investors when making investment decisions. Instead, they should focus on the trend. Livermore held the belief that opportunities thrive in all market conditions, and it is the responsibility of the investor to recognize and seize them. He was a true financial mercenary. Determining who was winning and switching to that side if needed. It taught me to have patience and trust, knowing that consistent and calculated decisions would pay off in the end.

John Maynard Keynes, a renowned economist and one of the most influential figures in modern economic theory, emphasized the importance of adapting to new information and changing circumstances in investment decision-making. Keynes believed investors should be open to revising their opinions and strategies when presented with additional facts or evidence. This principle reflects the dynamic nature of the financial markets and the need for investors to evaluate and adjust their positions constantly to stay ahead of changing market conditions.

Changing a point of view or outlook is a problem for many people. Making one decision was difficult enough, but to then reverse it and admit you made a mistake also becomes an issue of ego. Many people will dig in their heels at this point and employ the prayer tactic I mentioned before.

Keynes' principle encourages a proactive and responsive approach to portfolio management, allowing investors to take advantage of emerging opportunities and effectively mitigate risks. By staying adaptable and open-minded, investors can navigate the complexities of the financial markets more successfully and achieve long-term investment objectives.

Albert Einstein, a legendary physicist and Nobel laureate, offered a unique perspective on investment principles that emphasizes the importance of objectivity and rationality in decision-making. Einstein's principle underscores the need for investors to base their judgments on empirical evidence and logical reasoning rather than preconceived notions, biases, or tips. By focusing on the reality of the situation and avoiding wishful thinking, investors can make more informed and effective investment choices.

Einstein's principle highlights the psychological aspect of investing, acknowledging the impact of emotions and cognitive biases on decision-making. By adopting a disciplined and rational approach to investing, investors can overcome biases, such as confirmation bias, anchoring, and herd mentality, that can cloud judgment and lead to suboptimal outcomes. This principle reinforces the importance of objectivity and critical thinking in the investment process, enabling investors to achieve greater clarity and confidence in their decisions.

The investment principles of Jess Livermore, John Maynard Keynes, and Albert Einstein, which I employ, offer valuable insights and guidance for investors seeking to navigate the complexities of the financial markets. They serve as guideposts for our decisions in the ever-changing financial landscape. By integrating these principles into your investment strategies, investors can enhance their decision-making processes, manage risks more effectively, and achieve their long-term financial goals. While each principle has its own unique perspective and relevance, they collectively contribute to a holistic and well-rounded approach to investing that prioritizes flexibility, adaptability, and objectivity.

By embracing these principles and incorporating them into their investment philosophy, investors can and will cultivate a more resilient and sustainable approach to wealth management and achieve success in the ever-evolving world of finance. This approach emphasizes the importance of flexibility, critical thinking, and the ability to pivot when necessary. Investors can enhance their chances of success and achieve their financial goals. The wisdom of these influential figures continues to resonate with investors worldwide, reminding us of the timeless principles underpinning successful investing.

An example of where the mantras could have come in handy and where I should have followed my rules was a trade I made for my brother, Greg.

I had been observing the materials and precious metals sectors gradually rise in value and climb in the rankings of my lists. The precious metals sector, including the gold, silver, and base miners and explorers, had performed impressively and were about to give me a buy signal. I wanted to "front run" the position. Front running is when you get into a position before many other people get in. I wanted to be the first to what I felt would be a great party.

I should have waited, but I was impatient and maybe a little greedy. I wanted to help out my brother. I should have allowed it to move farther up the rankings. I broke my rules as I bought a precious metal fund for him in October 2012 at around $19.80. The security never made it any higher and drifted lower, so I sold it in January 2013 at around $16.30. Ophs. But at least I realized my mistake and got out of it. The fund, on May 18, 2017, was sitting at $11.33 and has never seen $19.80 since, or $16.30 for that matter.

By the way, I did get Greg into the GTAT trade, and he made some nice money.

You can see how each of these three mantras played an interlocking role in my decision to get out of the GTAT position. The stock had already fallen 22% from the high. The desire to let it climb back to the highs did not sway me. Even with a large and stable client like Apple, the price action wasn't acting that way. I

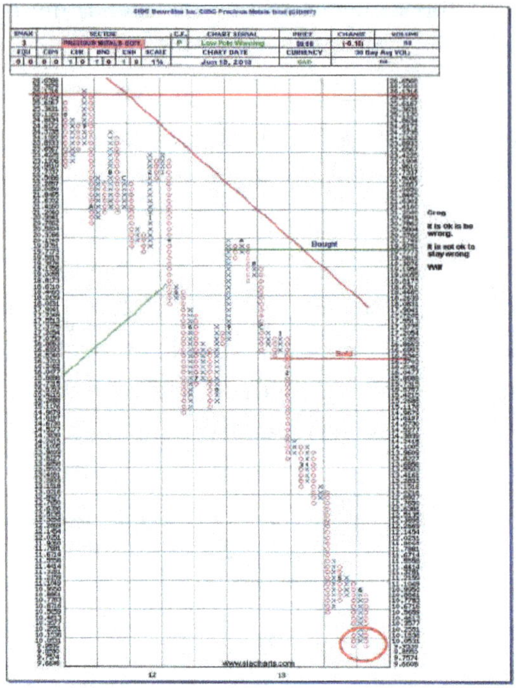

saw for what it was; a stock that was in decline, so I changed my mind.

For decades, researchers have been studying relative strength and momentum to see why it works and the conditions under which it works. They concluded it works under almost every circumstance.

I Believe

***** These are not just beliefs, they are the very essence of who I am. They form the very essence of my investment process and philosophy. The firm may not share these beliefs if you are a financial advisor or working with one. They will dissuade you with their own narratives. But I urge you to have the courage to look beyond and understand why these beliefs are crucial. Keep reading. *****

1 **I believe the true risk in investing lies not in losing money but in the potential of**

out living your money. Risk has changed because life has changed. People are looking forward to 30+ years of retirement, and during those 30 years, consumer prices will triple. So, the risk is not a loss of capital; it is the exhaustion of your purchasing power while you are still alive. We discuss this concept of risk in Chapter 12.

This means that the traditional notion of risk in investing has changed. In the past, the focus was on avoiding losses and preserving capital. While these are still important considerations, the greater risk lies in the erosion of purchasing power. Inflation can erode the value of your savings, making it harder to maintain your standard of living in retirement. You need to be prepared for this real, tangible risk.

Hence, having a long-term investment strategy that considers the potential impacts of inflation is crucial. A key part of this strategy is investing in assets that have historically outpaced inflation and taxes. Equities are the only asset that will fit this role.

In Chapter 12, we delve deeper into this concept of risk and provide strategies for managing and minimizing it. It's crucial for you, as a potential investor or someone planning for retirement, to be aware of the changing landscape of risk in investing and take proactive steps to address it. By doing so, you can better ensure a secure financial future for yourself and your loved ones. Remember, the true risk is not in losing money but in the possibility of outliving it. Let's work together to navigate these challenges and build a sustainable investment plan that will stand the test of time.

The concept of risk in investing is not just a theoretical construct but a crucial aspect that can profoundly alter your investment portfolio. In today's fast-paced world, investors are confronted with a diverse array of risks, from geopolitical upheavals to technological disruptions. It is imperative for investors to not only understand these risks but also have a robust plan in place to mitigate them. This understanding of risk is the cornerstone of successful investing. Not only must we be aware of the risks, but also our emotional reactions to their implications. More on this in Chapter 11. But before you skip ahead, continue reading.

Looking ahead, the future of risk in investing will likely be shaped by technological advancements, regulatory changes, and shifting global economic trends. It's crucial for investors to adapt to these changes and continue to evolve their risk management strategies to remain successful in the ever-changing world of investing. This dynamic nature of risk underscores the need for constant vigilance and adaptation in the investment landscape.

The concept of risk in investing is not a fixed notion but one that has evolved over time in response to our changing world. It is no longer solely about the potential loss of capital but about the ability to preserve and enhance your purchasing power in the face of shifting economic conditions.

2 I firmly believe that the ultimate security of financial investments lies in the continued accumulation of purchasing power. If the risk is the relentless erosion of purchasing power from inflation and taxes, then I define the accumulation of purchasing power as a positive return on my investment. Investments that offer this type of return are safe. Those who are not are not safe. By this definition, common stock is the safest long-term financial instrument.

As individuals, we all strive to make smart decisions about our finances to secure our future. We strive to earn our money through hard work and want to ensure that we invest it wisely for long-term growth. In this pursuit, it is crucial to consider how we can protect our investments from the relentless erosion of purchasing power caused by inflation and taxes. These investments ensure that our money maintains its value over time and continues to grow in real terms. This type of return is the true measure of financial security.

When considering the safety of different financial instruments, common stock stands out as one of the safest long-term investments. While stocks can be subject to market fluctuations and volatility in the short term, they have historically provided strong returns that have outpaced inflation and taxes over the long term. This makes them an excellent vehicle for building wealth and preserving purchasing power.

Furthermore, investing in diversified stocks allows for growth and protection against inflation, as company values tend to increase with time. Investing in a broad range of companies across various industries can mitigate risk and enhance one's chances of capturing the benefits of long-term economic growth. More on this in Chapters 14 and 15.

I cannot stress enough that the ultimate security of financial investments lies in the accumulation of purchasing power. We can safeguard our wealth and secure our financial future by ensuring that our investments provide a positive return that outpaces inflation and taxes. With its historical track record of generating strong returns over the long term, common stock remains one of the safest options for those seeking to preserve and grow their purchasing power. Through this prudent approach to investing, we can achieve true financial security.

3 I firmly believe that the great long-term risk of stocks is not owning them. When we look back at the historical events that have shaped our world, we see the incredible power of stocks to generate wealth and opportunities for growth. From the depths of the Great Depression to the highs of the modern stock market, the trajectory of the Dow Jones Industrial Average reminds us of the potential for long-term success in the stock market.

Take, for example, the intra-day low of the Dow Jones Industrial Average on July 8, 1932, at just 40 points. This was a time of immense economic hardship and uncertainty, with millions of Americans struggling to make ends meet. But those with the courage and wherewithal to invest in stocks during that tumultuous time were rewarded with incredible returns as the market began recovering.

Fast-forward to May 5, 2024, when the Dow Jones Industrial Average reached an all-time high of 40,077 points. Despite facing major challenges like World War II, the Cold War, the 9/11 terrorist attacks, and the COVID-19 pandemic, the stock market has continued to climb to new heights. This is a testament to the resilience and potential for growth that stocks can offer to investors who are willing to take the risk.

On a personal note, I had a front-row seat for Black Monday, October 19, 1987. The Dow Jones Industrial Average opened that day at 2,246 and closed at 1,738, losing 508 points or 23% in one day. I sat and watched in horror as the carnage ravaged everyone's accounts. There was no place to hide. Yet on January 24, 1989, the Dow closed above the opening of Black Monday and continued its upward climb.

I believe the right time to buy stocks is now if you have the means. While there may be short-term fluctuations in the market, history has shown us that stocks have the potential to generate significant returns over the long term. By investing in a diversified portfolio of stocks, you can position yourself to benefit from the growth of the global economy and the innovation of leading companies. In chapters 12 and 13, we will discuss this.

On the other hand, I also believe that the right time to sell stocks is never unless you have a pressing need for the money. Timing the market to sell stocks at the perfect moment is a risky and often futile endeavor. By holding onto your investments for the long term, you can ride out market fluctuations and benefit from the power of compound interest to grow your wealth over time.

To summarize this belief, the greatest risk of stocks is not owning them. By investing in stocks and holding onto them for the long term, you can potentially benefit from the growth of the market and secure your financial future. So, if you have the means to invest in stocks, now is the time to take advantage of the opportunities that the market has to offer. Don't let fear or uncertainty hold you back from reaching your financial goals.

We have a choice to make. We can have the assumed safety today in vehicles like bonds or Guaranteed Certificates of Deposit, which have little volatility and uncertainty tomorrow of having enough in the future because of inflation and taxes. Or we can have the volatility of equities today and live with the certainty of having enough assets that will beat inflation and taxes in the future. I choose equities today.

4 I believe everything you need to know about stock price movements can be summed up in these eight words: "The downs are temporary; the ups are permanent." I never see change or fluctuation as a loss. Stock prices fall all the time—about 25% every five years on average—but it doesn't matter because they never stay down. The market fluctuates but does not generate losses. Only humans can create a permanent loss by mistaking a temporary decline for a permanent recession and panic. **No Panic, No sell. No sell, No loss**. The enemy of investment success is not ignorance; it is fear. So, my **faith** and not my **knowledge** save my financial life, instilling confidence in the face of market volatility.

Fluctuation of the stock market is a fact of life in the world of investments. Many people may fear the ups and downs of the market, seeing it as a rollercoaster ride they want to get off of as soon as possible. They may wish to ride the merry-go-round. It seems safer, but you end up not going very far. It is crucial to understand that the stock market will inevitably fall at some point. However, instead of seeing this as a loss, it is important to view it as a natural part of the market cycle. The stock market will always recover from any temporary decline as the sun rises daily.

The real danger lies in our own reactions to market fluctuations. When panic sets in, it can lead to hasty decisions that result in permanent losses. Selling stocks in a panic only locks in any losses that may have occurred and prevents you from enjoying the long-term gains that inevitably come with market recovery.

The key to successful investing is faith in the market and your ability to weather any storm. Knowledge is important, but your confidence and resilience in the face of uncertainty will ultimately determine your financial success. By remembering that the downs are temporary and the ups are permanent, you can avoid the trap of fear and make decisions that are driven by reason and logic rather than emotion.

In conclusion, for this belief, believing in the mantra "The downs are temporary; the ups are permanent" is not just a philosophy, it is a strategy for financial success in the stock market.

By keeping faith in the market's resilience and avoiding the pitfalls of fear and panic, you can and will navigate market fluctuations confidently and come out on top in the long run. So, the next time you see a dip in stock prices, remember to stay calm, stay invested, and trust that the ups will always outweigh the downs in the end.

5 I process the experience, which most people describe as a "bear market" in two different words: "big sale." Since all declines are temporary, I regard all major generalized equity price declines as an opportunity to stock up on more truly safe investments before the sale ends. By taking advantage of lower prices during market declines, investors can purchase assets at a discount and potentially enjoy greater returns when the market eventually rebounds.

In times of economic turmoil, such as a bear market, it is natural for individuals to feel anxious and uncertain about their investments. Reframing the bear market experience as a "big sale" provides a unique opportunity to acquire high-quality assets at a discounted price.

While panicking and selling off investments during a market downturn may be tempting, believing you can reacquire your holdings at lower levels rarely happens. You end up having to make two decisions: when to sell and when to buy back again. I believe this reaction is counterproductive. Instead of viewing a bear market as a threat, I see it as a chance to capitalize on undervalued securities and secure a stronger financial position in the long run. This is the market's way of shaking out the weaker players. Don't let the emotions of the day drive your investment decisions.

A bear market presents a prime opportunity to bolster a portfolio with safe and reliable investments that may have been out of reach during more bullish market conditions. By maintaining a long-term perspective and staying disciplined in times of volatility, investors can position themselves for success and potentially outperform the market in the long.

I urge investors to resist the urge to liquidate their holdings during these trying times and instead consider leveraging this unique opportunity to acquire high-quality assets at a bargain price. By reframing the narrative of a bear market as a "big sale," we can turn a challenging market environment into a promising investment opportunity that holds the potential to create long-term wealth and financial security.

6 I don't believe in individual stocks; I believe in a managed portfolio of stocks. I can break a pencil; I cannot break 15 pencils tied together. That's diversification. Thus, one stock can go to zero, but stocks, as an asset class, can't go to zero.

The stock market has earned a reputation for its volatility and unpredictability throughout history. Some individual stocks have skyrocketed to new heights one day and plummeted to rock bottom the next. We use our relative strength techniques to avoid these types, yet this phenomenon has happened within our experience. This uncertainty has led many investors, including myself, to believe in the power of diversification through a managed portfolio of stocks.

When you buy only one stock, you are essentially putting all your eggs in one basket. If that stock takes a turn for the worse, you could stand to lose a significant portion of your investment. However, you are spreading the risk by diversifying your portfolio across various stocks and employing the strategies we encourage. Just as breaking one pencil is easy, breaking fifteen pencils tied together is much more difficult. This concept of diversification is what can protect your investments from the impact of a single stock going to zero.

It's important to recognize that while individual stocks may fail, stocks as an asset class are unlikely to go to zero. The stock market has historically trended upward over the long term despite short-term fluctuations. By investing in a managed portfolio of stocks, you are positioning yourself to benefit from the market's overall growth while minimizing the risk of any stock dragging down your entire investment.

A managed portfolio of stocks can reduce risk, provide greater stability, and potentially grow long-term. You will have the expertise and resources to carefully select and monitor a diverse range of stocks, optimizing your chances for success in the market. This level of professional insight can give you peace of mind.

I firmly believe that the key to successful investing lies in diversification through a managed portfolio of stocks. While individual stocks may have their ups and downs, a portfolio similar to what we recommend can help you weather the storm and achieve your financial goals in the long run. So why take unnecessary risks with your hard-earned money when you can trust in the power of diversification? Make the smart choice and invest in a managed portfolio of stocks today, using what you are learning here. Your future self will thank you.

More on how we accomplish this task in chapters 12 and 13. Or you can go directly to https://beyondetfspro.com

7 I love volatility. Volatility can't hurt me because I'm immune to panic. But it can help. First, higher volatility means (and is the price of) higher returns in an efficient market. Higher returns are good. Trust me on this.

Volatility is a term that often strikes fear into the hearts of investors. The idea of unpredictable and fluctuating markets can unsettle those who prefer stability and predictability. However, I am here to tell you that volatility is not something to be feared. In fact, I love volatility.

You see, volatility can't hurt me because I'm immune to panic. I have learned to embrace the ups and downs of the market with a calm and rational mindset. While others may run for the exits when things get rocky, I can see through the noise and maintain a long-term perspective on my investments.

But it's not just about staying calm in the face of market turbulence. Volatility can be actually a good thing for investors. In an efficient market, higher volatility is often associated with higher returns. This means that those who are willing to ride out the ups and downs of the market stand to benefit from potentially higher profits in the long run.

Higher returns are the ultimate goal of investing, and volatility is simply the price we pay for the opportunity to achieve them. It's like taking on a little bit of risk in order to potentially reap greater rewards. And trust me when I say that the potential rewards far outweigh the risks.

So the next time you see the market start to swing wildly, don't panic. Embrace the volatility and stay focused on the bigger picture. Remember that volatility can be your friend, not your enemy. Keep a cool head, stick to your investment strategy, and trust that higher returns are on the horizon.

I urge you to embrace volatility and all of the opportunities it presents. Stay calm, stay focused, and trust in the power of a well-thought-out investment strategy. With a little bit of courage and a lot of patience, you can navigate the ups and downs of the market with confidence and see your investments grow over time.

8 I'm not afraid of being in the next 25% downtick. I'm afraid of missing the next 100% uptick. I've tried and noticed that I cannot time the markets. Still, I have machined the risk of missing the next 100% uptick down to zero. It's called staying fully invested all the time. It works for me.

As investors, we all know the feeling of uncertainty regarding the stock market. There are ups and downs, highs and lows, and predicting what will happen next can be difficult. But one thing is certain - if you're not in the market, you're missing out on potential gains.

It's natural to fear the possibility of being in the next 25% downtick. Nobody wants to see their investments decrease in value. But what if I told you that the fear of missing the next 100% uptick should be even more concerning? Timing the markets is nearly impossible. Even the most experienced investors can't accurately predict when the next big jump will happen.

So, instead of trying to time the market, why not stay fully invested all the time? By staying fully invested, you eliminate the risk of missing out on potential gains. Sure, you may experience some downturns along the way, but the market has shown a history of growth over the long term. And by staying invested, you ensure you're along for the ride when that next 100% uptick comes around.

It's easy to let fear dictate your investment decisions, but staying fully invested can provide a sense of security and peace of mind. You're no longer worrying about missing out on opportunities or trying to time the market perfectly. Instead, you're letting your investments work for you and growing your wealth over time.

So why not take the fear out of investing and stay fully invested all the time? It may just be the key to achieving your financial goals and securing your financial future. Remember, it's not about timing the markets - it's about time in the markets. Stay invested, stay confident, and watch your wealth grow.

9 I do not believe in rebalancing portfolios. I believe in letting the markets determine that. We listen and act to the markets by implementing a relative strength strategy, not on some arbitrary target in time. It would be like saying you are going to cut grass when it is snowing out. It makes little sense; the weatherman is wrong, and so is re-balancing for me. Re-balancing, a practice recommended by financial advisors, is intended to keep your portfolio aligned with your investment goals and risk tolerance levels. I say that your risk tolerance level is your emotional response to the level of volatility. In an upmarket, we wish we had more; in a downmarket, we wish we didn't have so much. We understand that these feelings are part of the investment journey, and our strategy considers this emotional aspect.

Your risk tolerance is determined by a series of questions to determine where you sit on the efficient frontier. That is a mathematical formula that uses historical data and the questions you answered to determine your mix of different assets. In the chapter on risk, I will illuminate the fallacies found in this approach, providing you with a deeper understanding of the flaws in the traditional method. In fact, Harry Markowitz received the Nobel

Prize for his revolutionary investment theory by developing the Modern Portfolio Theory, with the efficient frontier as the cornerstone of his work. Later in his life, he admitted he does not follow his own work but has an allocation of 50% equities and 50% bonds. **Here, we have the creator of the mathematical formula for allocating your assets to optimize your asset mix for risk tolerance and for emotional factors that don't follow it.**

For a small subset of investors, primarily institutional in nature, the risk-related implications provide adequate justification for portfolio rebalancing. The only remaining considerations for this group pertain to the cost-minimizing implementation. Rebalancing to maintain constant weights constitutes an active contrarian strategy, particularly when details such as rebalancing frequency, tolerance bands, and other related factors are involved.

But what does 'rebalancing to constant weights' mean? It's a strategy that involves selling winners and buying losers to maintain a consistent portfolio composition. We have already shown the strong probability that in the particular time frame of 3-12 months, the winner will continue to win while the losing stocks will continue to lose. I do not wish to handicap myself with this type of strategy, and neither should you.

Constantly adjusting your portfolio could lead to unnecessary costs and hinder your ability to take advantage of market trends. Constantly buying and selling stocks can cause capital gains taxes, further reducing your overall profits.

10 I believe that, prior to retirement, people should own as close to 100% equities as they can emotionally stand. Then, after retirement, I believe they should own as close to 100% equities as they can emotionally stand. "Suitability" is a big issue, but it's an emotional issue, not a financial one. The emotional pull of bonds in retirement is very strong —— but systematic withdrawal from a stock portfolio makes more financial sense. Forget about income vs. principal for a moment, and think in terms of total returns. Would you rather have 4% a year from a portfolio of 4% bonds? Or would you rather take 8% from a portfolio of stocks (dividends and principal, let's say) whose index return is north of 10%? The latter way, your income has room to grow, and your principal has lots of room to grow. My belief is that, even in retirement, bonds are a non-starter.

As we approach retirement, there is often a shift in mindset towards more conservative investments, such as bonds. Investors believe bonds provide a stable source of income while preserving capital. However, this approach may not be the most effective to maximize returns and ensure financial security in retirement.

I advocate for owning as close to 100% equities as one can emotionally stand both before and after retirement. While this may seem like a risky strategy because of the stock market's volatility, the potential for higher returns outweighs the risks, especially in the long run.

When it comes to retirement planning, emotions often cloud rational decision-making. The fear of losing money can lead individuals to opt for conservative investments like bonds, even if they may not be the most financially prudent choice. However, it is important to consider the impact of inflation on the purchasing power of your savings over time.

By maintaining a portfolio of equities, you are positioning yourself for greater potential growth and higher total returns. Historically, the stock market has outperformed bonds in terms of long-term returns. Therefore, by investing in stocks, you are giving yourself the chance to grow your nest egg and potentially generate higher income in retirement.

The systematic withdrawal from a stock portfolio makes more financial sense. While bonds may offer a steady income stream, they may not keep up with the rising cost of living. Stocks have the potential to provide both income and capital growth, allowing for a more sustainable retirement income.

Remembering that retirement can span multiple decades, it becomes crucial to evaluate investments that offer enduring growth and stability. By maintaining a portfolio of equities, you are positioning yourself for a more financially secure retirement.

I believe that bonds are a non-starter in retirement planning. While they may offer a sense of security, they may not be the most effective way to ensure long-term financial stability. By owning as close to 100% equities as one can emotionally stand, both before and after retirement, individuals can maximize their potential for growth and income, ultimately leading to a more comfortable and secure retirement.

My business and life have to be run off my belief system and investment principles found in Chapters 6- 9. that's where my strength comes from, so I can't effectively help people who want to invest mostly in debt securities (see numbers 2 and 9). I can't effectively help people who want to buy single stocks (see number 6; I want to run portfolios of stocks). I can't help people effectively who want to go in and out of the markets (see number 8); it's impossible for individuals to do this well, and it misses the point (see numbers 3 and 4)

This is not hard. You got this. Let's continue.

Wilf Brockmann

10. Creating an Investor Mindset

Have you ever wondered what the keys to success in life are? What path do we need to tread? How do we get it? When do we arrive there? We all seek the secret formula, the golden pill, the elixir, that special sauce. The good news is, it's not a distant dream. Success is indeed attainable and is within our reach. We just haven't realized it yet. Yes, many will succumb to the shiny new object syndrome, or the grass is greener on the other side. I delve into these concepts further in the book. We can learn and model the attributes of success, which will inspire us to embark further on our journey of personal growth and take charge of our financial future. It will require some work, however, that we each have to do. We can't pay someone to do it for us. It is an individual experience that we can share with others, but ultimately, it's up to us to take the reins.

In the next two chapters, I intermingle mindset and emotions without hesitation in case anyone is keeping score. Sometimes, it is only a subtle difference, and I don't want to split hairs over it.

I define the investor's mindset as the internal dialogue and relationship we have between ourselves and our external environment. Yes, I talk to myself, and you should, too. There is also a dialogue between the two of me: myself, the true me, and my ego, who thinks he is me. These two are constantly in battle or conflict to be in control. We require them to be balanced so we can present ourselves as a united front to our external environment. Understanding this mindset is crucial as it empowers us to navigate the complexities of our trading experiences. I will go further into the ego in the next chapter, where we will discuss emotions and their impact on our lives and trading experiences.

Our objective and purpose is to understand ourselves, if possible, and to become more aware so that we can better relate to our surroundings and adapt when necessary. Let’s begin, shall we? Oh, by the way, smile.

When you think about your most recurring and costly trading mistakes, they’re probably related to common errors, such as chasing prices, cutting winners short, holding on to losers, forcing mediocre trades, and over-trading. You may have tried to fix these errors by improving your technical skills, and yet they persist. That’s because the actual source of these mistakes is not technical—they actually stem from greed, fear, anger, or problems with confidence and lack of discipline. If you are like most investors, you probably overlook or misunderstand mental and emotional obstacles. Or worse, you might think you know how to manage them but don’t and lose control at the worst possible time.

The Power of Mindfulness in Investing

It is easy to get swept up in the chaos of the markets. However, by incorporating mindfulness, investors can tap into the power of the present moment to make more informed and strategic decisions. Mindfulness isn't just a philosophical concept; it's a practical tool for understanding our thoughts and emotions and being fully present in each moment without judgment or attachment to outcomes. We'll be delving into this practical approach in the next chapter, as it's a crucial starting point for decision-making.

By incorporating mindfulness into our investment program, we can cultivate a sense of calm and clarity that will help us navigate the market's ups and downs with grace and resilience. Instead of reacting impulsively to market fluctuations, mindfulness allows us to pause, breathe, and assess the situation before making a decision. This level-headed approach can lead to more thoughtful and deliberate investment choices, ultimately leading to greater success in the long run. It's a strategy that will reassure you and boost your confidence in your decisions.

What's that sound? Do you hear it? No, seriously, what's that sound? Unless it is the sound of a fire alarm, someone crying, or danger, we ignore it. We need to do the same in our trading environment. Ignore it unless it is specific to me, my portfolio, or my strategy. XYZ is up 10 percent today!! Do I own it? No. Was I going to buy it? No. So why get so worked up? Yes, my ego will say to me, "We should have bought it, I was thinking about it? Just tell your ego to relax and instead tell it, "Wow, someone is going to be happy they own it."

Practicing mindfulness can help us develop greater self-awareness and emotional intelligence. By tuning into our thoughts and feelings as they arise, we can gain valuable insights into our biases and triggers that may affect our investment decisions. This heightened self-awareness can help us avoid making impulsive or emotionally driven trades again, leading to more consistent and profitable outcomes in the long run. Writing them down and then later reviewing helps in this process.

One crucial element in this process is our becoming self-awareness. As Sun Tzu wisely said, "*Know the enemy and know yourself.*" Awareness of our surroundings and situation is not just a key; it's a superpower. Many of us will stumble into a situation. In the next chapter, we will delve into the significance of this factor in our decision-making process.

One pivotal advantage of mindfulness is the capacity to tune into our intuition and gut instincts. By silencing the noise of external distractions and focusing on the present moment, we can tap into our inner wisdom and make decisions that resonate with our values and goals. This intuitive approach can help us steer clear of impulsive and fear-based decisions and instill a sense of trust in our judgment and expertise. Did my intuition kick into high gear when I saw the sell signal on GTAT?

Our ability to be mindful and present enhances our investment strategy. By cultivating a calm and focused mindset, we can make more informed decisions, tap into our intuition, and navigate market fluctuations with grace and resilience. We can enhance our financial success and cultivate a sense of inner peace and well-being that will serve us well in all areas of our lives.

If we are not self-aware, we will end up patching leaky holes in the boat rather than charting the course forward. When one becomes self-aware, the residual effect is being in the present. I do not fret about the past or worry about the future; I am totally present in the here and now. That is at least our object.

Cultivating Patience and Discipline in Trading

These are the springboard to freedom. Cultivating patience and discipline is unquestionably one key in our quest for success. As investors, it's easy to get caught up in the market's excitement and make impulsive decisions. However, by practicing mindfulness and staying grounded in the present moment, we can develop the patience and discipline needed to make wise investment choices. Chasing XYZ when it is not part of our plan is not worth it.

The mindset we need is one that is strongly anchored in the present. Yes, it can be challenging. Many distractions can and will pull us away from our investment goals and objectives. However, to maintain our focus on tasks that may seem mundane, we need discipline, discipline to stay on track and adhere to the plan. This may require significant mental energy, but it is the driving force that propels us towards success. In a constantly changing market, chasing quick profits or panicking when things don't go our way can be tempting. However, practicing mindfulness can teach us to embrace uncertainty and trust in the process and our rules rather than succumb to fear or greed. This patience and discipline will serve us well as we navigate the currents of the market with grace and resilience.

What are the benefits of doing this? We can experience greater peace, clarity, and confidence in our decision-making process. By staying present, self-aware, and disciplined, we can create a more harmonious and successful relationship with the stock market, allowing us to achieve our financial goals while also nurturing our own well-being. So take a moment to pause, breathe, smile and reflect on how mindfulness can transform your approach to investing, and watch as your portfolio flourishes in the light of your newfound wisdom and serenity. This does not mean you fall asleep in a state of bliss but rather are aware of what is going on around you.

Patience is essential in trading because the market can be unpredictable and volatile. It's important to remember that investing is a long-term game, and success doesn't happen overnight. It would be nice if it were, but it is not. By staying patient and not getting caught up in the market's highs and lows, we can make more rational decisions that will benefit us in the long run. Patience does not mean doing nothing. It is a state of observing and studying. Many traders feel they have to be active. You can be active in your research and observation. Action for the sake of action is not a correct and proper path to follow.

By combining patience and the required discipline in our practices, we will achieve a sense of balance and harmony in our investment strategy and also in our lives. This allows us to approach the market with a rational mind and decide based on logic and reason rather than emotion. We will then navigate the market's trials with grace and poise rather than moving forward with a jolting movement.

Overcoming Emotional Reactions to Market Volatility

Market volatility is the most common occurrence that can and will trigger strong emotional reactions in even the most seasoned investors. When the market takes a dip, it's easy to let fear and panic dictate our decisions, leading to impulsive actions that can harm our portfolio in the long run. In contrast, when the market is rising, we can feel euphoric and feel the need to add more capital. We require the discipline to overcome these emotional reactions and make decisions that align with our long-term goals.

Besides enhancing decision-making skills, mindfulness can also improve overall mental well-being and emotional resilience in the face of market volatility. By practicing techniques such as meditation, deep breathing, and visualization, investors can cultivate a sense of inner peace and balance that will help them weather the inevitable storms of the stock market. This sense of inner strength and stability can provide a solid foundation for making sound investment choices, even in challenging times.

When I face market volatility, I try to take a step back and recognize the emotions that are arising within me. Am I feeling anxious, fearful, or excited? By acknowledging these emotions without reacting to them, you can better understand our mindset and how it may influence our investment decisions.

Investing is a solo sport. We are not competing against others but against ourselves. You will realize that self-satisfaction is a lot more profitable and rewarding than gloating. Leave the gloating for the golf course. I will repeat many times throughout our journey about the emotions of fear and greed.

Practicing gratitude is another mindfulness technique that can help us overcome emotional reactions. When the market is turbulent, it's easy to focus on what you may lose rather than what you still have. Take a moment to reflect on all the positive aspects of your investments and the opportunities that market volatility may present. By cultivating a sense of gratitude, we can shift our perspective from scarcity to abundance, empowering us to make more rational and strategic decisions. A dash of humility is also helpful in overcoming the situation. Self-pity focuses our attention on ourselves and not on where it should be. Focus on what's out there, not on yourself. See what is happening around you. It takes courage to take the spotlight off yourself.

This can also help us develop resilience in the face of market volatility. By cultivating a mindset of acceptance and non-attachment to outcomes, we can weather the market's difficulties with greater ease. Remember that market fluctuations are a natural part of investing and trading, and by staying grounded in the present moment, we can maintain a sense of calm and clarity that will guide us through turbulent times. Yes, smiles help as well.

By applying these techniques to our investment program and systems, we can cultivate a sense of inner peace and confidence that will serve us well in navigating the unpredictable nature of the stock market. By acknowledging our emotions, practicing gratitude, being humble, and developing resilience, we can and will overcome emotional reactions to market volatility and make more mindful investment decisions that align with our long-term goals. Trust, stay present at the moment, and remember that with mindfulness, you have the power to achieve stock market Zen. "*Ya, Ya*", I can hear you saying, "*I got this.*" Oh, just make sure you really do have it.

Setting Clear Written Goals and Intentions for Our Investments

Clear, written goals are essential for success in all aspects of life, whether in your personal life, career, academic pursuits, or, most importantly, your financial life. Defined goals can provide a roadmap to achieving our dreams. Having written goals let us prioritize our efforts and energies on what matters. When you take the time to write your goals, you are essentially committing yourself to working towards achieving them. It creates a setting where accountability is required on our part. This commitment helps you stay motivated and determined, even when faced with obstacles or setbacks. Setting a goal of making money is too open-ended. How will you know when you have achieved it? Once you met a milestone, remember to celebrate and then go on to the next target.

Create a timeline for achieving your goals by breaking them down into smaller, manageable tasks. This not only helps you stay on track but also allows you to celebrate your accomplishments along the way. Seeing tangible progress towards your goals can boost your confidence and motivation, propelling you to keep working towards your ultimate objectives. Have big goals and then a number of smaller ones. They don't have to be related, even as odd as "I will not look at my phone for 30 minutes". If unsuccessful, drop it down to 20 minutes. Achieving little goals provides us with the confidence that the big ones can be met as well.

Setting clear investment goals allows us to stay focused and aligned with our values, ultimately leading to more successful outcomes in the long run. When setting our investment goals, it is essential to take the time to reflect on what truly matters. What are our financial aspirations? What are our values and beliefs about money and investing? By answering these questions honestly, you can create goals that are achievable and meaningful to us on a deeper level. This mindfulness approach will guide us toward making investment decisions that align with our values and beliefs.

It is also important to establish intentions for our investments. What are these funds to be used for? Having goals and intentions for our investments will also help us stay disciplined and avoid making impulsive decisions based on emotions or short-term market trends. By staying true to your goals and intentions, you can maintain a long-term perspective and make informed decisions that are in line with your overall investment strategy.

Without clear goals, it is easy to lose sight of what you are working towards and become distracted by other, less important tasks. Written goals help to provide direction and clarity in your decision-making process. When you have a clear vision of what you want to achieve, making decisions that align with your goals becomes easier. This can help you avoid wasting time and energy on activities that do not bring you closer to your desired outcome, keeping you focused and attentive.

Setting clear, written goals can improve your time management skills. When you clearly understand what you want to achieve, you can prioritize your tasks and allocate your time effectively. This can help you avoid procrastination and stay organized, leading to increased productivity and efficiency.

Having these written goals is essential for success in all areas of life; they provide a sense of purpose and direction, help you make informed decisions, allow you to track your progress, and improve your time management skills. By defining your goals and writing them down, you are setting yourself up for success and increasing your chances of achieving your dreams. So, what are you waiting for? Grab a pen and paper, and start setting clear, written goals today! Remember, mindfulness and intentionality are key ingredients to achieving stock market Zen.

Staying Committed to Your Investment Goals with Mindful Persistence

Now that you have your goals down on paper staying committed is crucial. One way to stay committed to our investment goals is to review and reassess our portfolio regularly. Take the time to reflect, evaluate your performance, and make any necessary adjustments to stay on track. By staying proactive and engaged with, you can ensure that you are always moving towards your financial goals.

Another key aspect of persistence is staying positive and maintaining a sense of optimism, even in the face of challenges or setbacks. Not that you should always be excessively happy—that is not reality. Just don't be a downer all the time. It distracts both you and those around you. By staying focused on our goals and maintaining a positive mindset, we can weather any storms and continue to make progress towards financial success.

Setting personal development goals is a must, and I don't mean to set them and leave them. As investors, it's important to constantly strive for self-improvement to succeed in this competitive field. Setting specific and measurable goals allows you to track your progress and stay motivated to push yourself to new heights. Remember, personal development is a journey, not a destination, so embrace the process and enjoy the growth that comes with it.

One key aspect of setting personal development goals is to focus on improving your trading psychology and mindset. This includes working on managing your emotions, developing discipline, and cultivating a positive attitude towards your trading activities. By setting goals such as practicing mindfulness, journaling your thoughts and emotions, and seeking feedback from mentors or peers, you can enhance your mental strength and resilience in the face of market fluctuations and challenges.

Another important factor to consider when setting personal development goals is to align them with your long-term vision and values as an investor. Take the time to reflect on what truly matters to you in your trading journey and set goals that are in line with your core beliefs and aspirations. This will help you stay motivated and focused on your path to success, even when faced with setbacks or obstacles along the way.

As you embark on your personal development journey, remember to celebrate your successes and learn from your failures. Even if you stay away from your phone for only 30 minutes, every experience, whether positive or negative, is an opportunity for growth and learning. By staying open to new possibilities and being willing to adapt and evolve, you can continue to progress and thrive in the dynamic world of trading and investing.

Mindful Breathing Exercises for Stress Reduction

Focusing on our breath allows us to ground ourselves in the present moment and cultivate a sense of calm amidst the chaos. It is so easy to get rattled by, in many cases, minor things. To begin a mindful breathing exercise, find a quiet space where you can sit comfortably and close your eyes. Take a few deep breaths to settle into your body and bring your attention to the sensation of the air entering and leaving your nostrils. Notice the rise and fall of your chest with each inhale and exhale. As thoughts or distractions arise, simply acknowledge them and gently guide your attention back to your breath.

As you continue to practice mindful breathing, you may notice a sense of relaxation washing over you. By tuning into your breath, you can quiet the chatter of your mind and create a sense of inner peace. This can be especially beneficial during times of market volatility when emotions can run high and cloud your judgment. You can regain clarity and make more informed decisions by taking a few moments to focus on your breath.

Mindful breathing exercises can also help you cultivate resilience in the face of uncertainty. By learning to stay present with your breath, you can train your mind to stay calm and centered, even when the market is in turmoil. This sense of inner strength will benefit not only your investment strategy but also your overall well-being. Remember, the market will always have its ups and downs, but by practicing mindfulness, you can weather the storm with grace and confidence.

Incorporating mindful breathing exercises into your daily routine is a powerful way to reduce stress, enhance focus, and promote emotional well-being. Take a few moments each day to connect with your breath and cultivate a sense of mindfulness. By doing so, you can approach your investments with clarity, confidence, and a sense of inner peace. Embrace the power of mindful breathing and watch as your investment strategy transforms into a practice of Zen-like calmness and resilience.

Mindful Observation of Market Trends and Patterns

Mindful observation involves paying attention to the present moment without judgment, allowing you to make more informed decisions based on real-time data rather than emotional reactions. For example, when I spoke about reading the tape, if we open our minds and our eyes, we become more aware of subtle changes in the fabric of the markets. Traders can spot unusual activity and detect the beginning of patterns.

By staying in the present and aware of what is happening around us, we can better expect shifts and make strategic moves to maximize our returns; we become attuned to subtle fluctuations and signals. This level of mindfulness allows us to see beyond the noise and distractions of the market, giving us a deeper understanding of the underlying dynamics at play. By approaching market analysis with a calm and focused mindset, we can connect the dots between unrelated data points and uncover valuable insights. By maintaining a heightened awareness, we can gain a competitive edge in the market and spot opportunities before they are recognized. One issue to be careful about is not to see patterns that don't exist. This is so easy a trap to fall for. A lot of this is ego-driven. Just tell him to take a back seat and enjoy the ride, and if you need his assistance, he will be called upon.

Awareness of patterns as they develop differs from seeing patterns that don't exist. Read further when I talk about rats beating out us humans, and you will understand what I am talking about. Having a rules-based trading plan like the one we have with Beyond ETFs will simplify much of this.

We can improve our decision-making by trusting our instincts and staying grounded in the present moment. Incorporating mindfulness into our investment strategy is not just about making money, it's about cultivating a deeper sense of awareness and connection with your surroundings. By observing market trends and patterns attentively, we can tap into a source of wisdom beyond mere numbers and statistics. So take a breath, center yourself, and approach your investments with a clear and focused mind. The rewards will not only be financial but also spiritual and emotional as you learn to navigate the market with a sense of calm and presence.

Incorporating Mindful Meditation into Your Daily Routine

Incorporating meditation into your daily routine is powerful. You can develop a greater sense of clarity, focus, and emotional resilience by quieting your mind and focusing on the present moment. Mindful meditation can help you stay calm and centered in the face of market fluctuations, enabling you to make more rational and informed choices. In my practice, I engage in Christian meditation for 20 minutes in the morning and 20 minutes in the evening. It doesn't matter what type of meditation you try, but this works for me. We strive to create an environment in which we are in harmony with our center.

The essence of meditation is to let go of the ego. We are not seeing what is happening with the ego. Its self-centeredness limits the self-view. The eye with which we see without limit is the eye that does not see itself. The paradox of meditation is that when we stop trying to see and have, we see everything, and everything is ours. To do this, we learn to be quiet, silent, and truly humble. It requires discipline and patience.

Begin by setting aside a few minutes daily. Find a quiet space where you can sit comfortably with your back erect and focus on your breath. Close your eyes, take deep breaths, and bring your attention to the sensations of your breath moving in and out of your body. Pick one word as your mantra and repeat it slowly. As you practice this simple exercise, you will begin to cultivate a sense of inner peace and stillness that can carry over into your investment decisions. Build up the time you devote to this endeavor to 20 minutes in each session. Practice twice a day; morning and evening.

The purpose of saying the mantra is that it becomes the focus of your attention. We are not thinking of anything or pursuing any insights that may come to us as we say the mantra. Let all your thoughts fall away as you come to an ever deeper silence in which the only sound in your mind is the mantra. The mantra itself will teach you the patience needed to say it. It will also teach you the humility needed. In meditating, we do not seek to possess God or to arrive at a profound insight into God. We are simply seeking to accept the gift of our creation as fully as we presently can and respond to it as generously as we can.

You may find that you are better able to manage the stress and anxiety that can sometimes accompany the market and life itself. By developing a sense of mindfulness, you can learn to observe your thoughts and emotions without becoming overwhelmed by them. This can give you the clarity and perspective you need to make sound investment choices based on logic and reason rather than fear or impulsivity.

Besides enhancing your emotional well-being, mindful meditation can also improve your overall cognitive function. By training your mind to focus on the present moment, you can sharpen your ability to analyze data, identify trends, and make strategic decisions for your investment portfolio. With a clear and focused mind, you can approach the market with a sense of confidence and competence that will serve you well in your trading activities.

As you continue to practice mindfulness meditation, you find that your investment strategy becomes more grounded, rational, and effective, leading to greater prosperity and fulfillment in your financial journey.

Using Mindfulness to Avoid Impulsive Trading Decisions

Getting caught up in the excitement and making impulsive trading decisions is easy, believe me. Sometimes, they work out, but most times, they do not. We can avoid falling victim to these impulsive tendencies. Your sense of self-awareness needs to be nurtured and developed, allowing you to pay attention to your thoughts and emotions. With this, you can identify patterns or triggers that may lead to impulsive trading decisions. Once you are aware of these tendencies, you can take steps to address them and make more deliberate choices for your investments. Stay present in the moment and maintain focus on the long-term goals.

Incorporating these may take time and practice, but the benefits can be profound. By staying present, self-aware, patient, and disciplined, you can avoid impulsive trading decisions and make more informed choices, which will ultimately lead to greater success in the stock market. So take a moment to breathe, center yourself, and approach your investments with a clear and focused mind. Your portfolio will thank you for it.

Finding Peace and Tranquility in Your Investment Journey

As an investor, it is crucial to find moments of peace and tranquility amidst the constant fluctuations and uncertainties. One of the first steps to finding peace and tranquility is to practice mindfulness meditation. Taking just a few minutes each day to quiet your mind and focus on the present moment can help you develop a greater sense of awareness and concentration. By grounding yourself in the here and now, you can better navigate the trials of the stock market with equanimity and composure.

Another key aspect is to let go of attachment to outcomes. While having goals and aspirations for our investments is natural, becoming too fixated on specific outcomes can lead to unnecessary stress and anxiety. By practicing detachment and accepting whatever results may come, we can approach our investment decisions with a sense of openness and flexibility, allowing for greater adaptability in the face of uncertainty. This does not mean you allow continued failures to achieve your targets to go unattended. You review and correct. A plane flying from New York to Las Angeles might be on auto-pilot most of the way, but it is continuing to fine-tune its approach to stay on course. It is adapting to the changes as they occur. We need to as well.

Again, incorporating mindfulness techniques such as deep breathing, body scanning, and visualization can also help you stay grounded and centered during turbulent times. Tuning into your body and breathing can release tension and anxiety, allowing for a greater sense of relaxation and peace. Visualizing successful outcomes and positive affirmations can also help boost your confidence and resilience in the face of challenges. We need to cultivate a sense of balance and harmony between our mind, body, and spirit and the external world.

Embracing the Uncertainty of the Stock Market with Mindful Awareness

Uncertainty is our constant companion today. Prices can change, news can break anytime, and emotions can run high. Getting caught up in the chaos can be easy, and we can let fear or greed drive our decisions. However, we can navigate these turbulent waters with grace and poise by embracing the uncertainty. We know it is there. Give it space, and don't be surprised when it develops. I am more worried when things are calm and flat. I become too relaxed and end up putting my feet up and then snoozing.

Mindfulness is the practice of embodying complete presence and awareness of the moment without judgment. It's not just a philosophical concept but a practical tool that can help you stay grounded and focused, even when the market is in turmoil. This can help us make more rational and informed decisions rather than reacting hastily to market fluctuations, making you feel more prepared and equipped.

Embracing the uncertainty means letting go of the need for certainty. It would be nice to be certain, but it is unnecessary. This is indeed difficult to do. The market is inherently unpredictable, and attempting to control or predict its movements is a futile endeavor. Instead, we can cultivate a sense of peace and calm in the face of volatility by accepting the market's uncertainty and impermanence, making you feel more at peace with the market's unpredictability.

Practicing mindfulness can also help us better understand our motivations and biases. By observing our thoughts and emotions without judgment, we can become more aware of how fear, greed, or other emotions may influence our decisions. This self-awareness can help you make more objective and rational choices, leading to more successful investment outcomes.

Embracing A Stock Market Zen in Your Investment

Embracing a Stock Market Zen in our investment journey means cultivating a mindset of mindfulness and peace in our trading practices. By reflecting on our investment practices, we can better understand our motivations and reactions to market fluctuations. This self-awareness can help us make more informed decisions and stay grounded during times of volatility. It is essential to recognize that the stock market is ever-changing and requires a constant presence of mind. By embracing the peace and fulfillment of the Stock Market Zen, we can experience a sense of harmony and balance in our investment strategy.

Staying calm and focused is hard but necessary. By taking a step back and observing our thoughts and feelings during trading, we can cultivate clarity and objectivity in our decision-making process.

Embracing peace and fulfillment is about finding a sense of contentment and satisfaction in our investment journey. By letting go of attachment to outcomes and focusing on the present moment, we can experience a deeper connection to our trading practices. When we approach the market with a sense of peace and fulfillment, we can make decisions that align with your values and long-term goals. Ultimately, the Stock Market Zen is not just about making money, but about finding joy and purpose in the process of investing.

"You don't need to be a rocket scientist. Investing is not a game where the guy with a 160 IQ beats the guy with a 130 IQ. Rationality is essential.—Warren Buffett

11. ~~War~~ Emotions, what is it good for? Absolutely nothing, listen to me."

Just as Edwin Star's 1970s anti-Vietnam song 'War' remains a poignant protest song against the destruction and devastation of war, emotions can be equally destructive in the world of financial trading. Like war, emotional trading can lead to significant financial losses. It's crucial to be aware of these additional risks and take steps to manage them. Emotions deal with the internal struggles we face and have to deal with.

Emotions play a crucial role in the world of trading. As traders, it is essential to understand the significance of emotions in making profitable decisions. Emotions such as fear, greed, and excitement can often cloud our judgment and lead to impulsive actions that may not be in our best interest. However, when harnessed correctly, emotions can also be powerful tools in guiding us towards successful trades.

One key reason emotions are important in trading is that they provide valuable insights into market sentiment. By being aware of our own emotions and how market conditions influence them, we can better understand the collective emotions of other traders. This awareness can help us expect market movements and make more informed decisions. Emotions can act as a compass, guiding us towards opportunities we may have overlooked.

Emotional issues were and are still a significant hurdle to my trading journey. However, I am learning to manage them better. When I reviewed my trading journal, emotional reactions were a major cause of the trade failure. For me, a losing trade is not a failure if it aligns with the trading plan. A good trade is one in which I follow the rules. This personal experience underscores the importance of managing emotions while trading. How can losing trade not be a failure? Simple, if the trading plan calls for its removal from the portfolio. The portfolio I run for the Beyond ETFs Pro model has accumulated 493 trades in total from 2 January 2007 to 30 June 2024. Of those trades, 245 were winning, 248 were losing. It generated a return of 20.21% per year during that period. The S&P 100 only generated a return of 8.25%. To learn more about this program and how to participate, visit https://beyondetfspro.com.

The main reason for not following my and, most likely, your trading plan is emotions. Laziness comes a close second. Maintaining a clear and rational mindset is important. When we allow emotions to take control, we are more likely to make impulsive decisions based on fear, greed, or panic. These emotions can lead to irrational trading choices that result in significant losses. However, by keeping emotions in check and following a well-thought-out trading plan, we can avoid making reckless decisions that can and will harm our trading accounts. This is the reason I encourage you to look at the premise behind The Brockmann Method embodied in the Beyond ETFs Pro app. We will discuss further how it works and how you can benefit by implementing this strategy, potentially leading to significant financial success that can transform your trading experience and give you a new level of confidence in your abilities.

Emotions can also serve as a source of motivation and drive. When we are passionate about what we do and truly engaged in the trading process, our emotions can fuel our determination and perseverance. Emotions can help us stay focused and committed to our goals, even in the face of challenges and setbacks.

In addition, emotions can also be a source of inspiration and creativity in our trading strategies. When we allow ourselves to tap into our emotions, we can think outside the box and come up with innovative approaches to trading. Emotions can help us see opportunities where others see obstacles and can inspire us to take calculated risks that lead to greater rewards. By embracing our emotions and using them to our advantage, we can set ourselves apart from the crowd and achieve greater success.

Understanding Your Emotional Triggers

Understanding your emotional triggers can help you control your reactions to different situations. One of the first steps in understanding trigger points is to identify them. Note the situations or events that cause you to feel anxious or overconfident. By recognizing these triggers, you can develop strategies to manage them more effectively. You require this self-awareness to maintain a clear and focused mindset while trading. Make notes, "I did this, and this is what happened." But don't beat yourself up too much.

Once you have identified your emotional triggers, it's important to explore their underlying reasons. Are you reacting out of fear of losing money, or are you feeling overly confident in a winning streak? By delving deeper into the root causes of your emotions, you can address them more effectively. This introspection will help you develop a healthier relationship with your emotions and make more rational decisions when trading.

Besides understanding your emotional triggers, it's also important to develop coping mechanisms to manage them. This could include techniques such as deep breathing exercises, mindfulness practices, or taking a break from trading when you feel overwhelmed. By having these tools at your disposal, you can better navigate the trials of the market without letting your emotions cloud your judgment.

Procrastination is an avoidance skill. Not dealing with a situation effectively and quickly will most likely result in it leading to becoming unmanageable. Should you make a market error, for example, cover it immediately and move on. Don't try to trade your way out of it. Take the loss, learn to be more careful, and move on. Deal with the little things before they become the bigger things.

Understanding our emotional triggers and developing strategies to manage them can help us become more disciplined and successful traders. Embrace the journey of self-discovery and emotional growth, knowing that by mastering your emotions, you are setting yourself up for long-term success in the world of trading. Remember, the key to profitable trading lies in market analysis and understanding and mastering your own psychology.

Overcoming Fear and Greed

The emotions of fear and greed have a strong impact on our level of success. These emotions can cloud our judgment, leading to impulsive decisions that may not be in our best interest. One of the first steps to overcoming these is to recognize when these emotions are at play. Fear often manifests as a reluctance to take risks or a hesitation to decide. Greed can lead to overconfidence and a willingness to take unnecessary risks. By being aware of these emotions and how they affect your decision-making process, we can take steps to counteract their influence. We cover risk avoidance in greater detail further on.

One effective way is to develop a solid trading plan. Having a clear set of rules and strategies in place can help us make informed decisions based on logic rather than emotion. By sticking to our plan and not allowing fear or greed to sway your actions, we can avoid making impulsive and harmful decisions.

Another key to overcoming fear and greed is to cultivate a mindset of patience and discipline. Remember that trading is a marathon, not a sprint, and that success in the market takes time and dedication. By staying focused on our long-term goals and remaining disciplined in our trading approach, we can avoid falling victim to the emotional rollercoaster of fear and greed.

Managing Losses and Avoiding Revenge Trading

Losses are inevitable in our world of trading. No matter how experienced or skilled you are, there will always be times when the market goes against you. How you manage these losses will ultimately determine your success as a trader. Instead of letting losses consume you with anger and frustration or getting you down, it is important to approach them with a level head and a rational mind.

One key way to manage losses is to avoid revenge trading. Revenge trading is when you try to recoup your losses by taking risky and impulsive trades. Doubling down on an already losing trading will not work. Believe me when I say this. This can be a dangerous cycle that often leads to even bigger losses. Instead of letting your emotions take control, stepping back and reassessing your trading strategy is crucial. Take a break, analyze what went wrong, and make appropriate adjustments. I have a rule. If I have had three unsuccessful trades in a row and losses, I will step away and halt trading for the day. That holds true with three successful trades as well. The odds are that emotions are going to come into play, and it is not going to be pretty for my bottom line.

It is important to remember that losses are a natural part of trading. No trader, no matter how successful, is immune to them. The key is to accept them as a learning opportunity and not as a personal failure. By viewing losses in this way, you can grow and improve as a trader. Remember, every successful trader has faced losses in their career—how they bounce back from them sets them apart. I point out again that the Beyond ETFs portfolio has had more losses than winners yet has generated a return of 20.21% per year for the last 17 ½ years. Cut the losers short and let the winners ride. On average, we held winners for 175.64 days, while we only held losers for 63.96 days.

Another crucial aspect of managing losses is to set clear risk management rules. This means defining how much you are willing to risk on each trade and sticking to that limit. Setting these boundaries can protect your capital and prevent emotional decision-making.

By sticking to your plan and not letting emotions cloud your judgment, you can stay focused on your goals and objectives. A well-thought-out trading plan can also help you manage risk effectively and minimize potential losses. This approach is also less stressful, and the pivot points and decision facts are already in place. You just have to follow the plan and smile.

Seeking Feedback and Continuous Improvement

Seeking feedback and continuous improvement are crucial aspects of becoming a successful trader. In the fast-paced world of trading, it's easy to get caught up in the excitement of the markets and lose sight of the bigger picture. However, by actively seeking feedback from others and constantly striving to improve your skills, you can set yourself apart from the competition and achieve greater success in your trading endeavors. Seeking feedback or help is, again, not a sign of weakness. Why recreate the wheel when someone has already done that for you?

Furthermore, it is important to surround yourself with a supportive network of fellow traders, investors and family. By sharing ideas and strategies with like-minded individuals, you can gain valuable insights and perspectives to help you make better decisions. Learning from the experiences of others can also help you avoid common pitfalls and mistakes in the market. Building a strong community of traders can enhance your decision-making skills and help you stay motivated and inspired on your trading journey. My group is called the Band of Brothers. Sisters are welcome as well. We are a group of traders who share our insights and thoughts among ourselves. They are not afraid to call out fellow members for their faulty perspectives and assumptions, for which I am grateful.

Feedback is a powerful tool that can help you identify your strengths and weaknesses as a trader. By seeking feedback from trusted mentors, colleagues, or even from your own performance data, you can gain valuable insights into areas where you excel and where you can improve. Instead of seeing feedback as criticism, embrace it as an opportunity to learn and evolve as a trader.

Continuous improvement is the key to long-term success in the world of trading as well as in life. As the markets evolve and change, it is essential that you also evolve and adapt your strategies and mindset. By constantly seeking out new information, learning from your mistakes, and refining your trading techniques, you can stay ahead of the curve and increase your profitability. Remember, trading is a journey, not a destination, and each day presents new opportunities for growth and improvement.

The road to success in trading is not always easy, and there will undoubtedly be challenges and setbacks along the way. However, by approaching each obstacle as an opportunity to learn and grow, you can turn even the most difficult situations into valuable learning experiences. Embrace seeking feedback and continuous improvement as a chance to become the best trader you can be, and never stop striving for excellence in your craft.

Remember, the journey to success is a marathon, not a sprint, so stay committed to your growth and development as a trader, and the results will follow.

Building Resilience in the Face of Adversity

Facing adversity is inevitable. Whether it's a sudden market crash, a failed trade, or a personal setback, challenges will arise that test our resolve and mental fortitude. Resilience is the ability to bounce back from setbacks, adapt to change, and persevere in the face of adversity. It is a quality that separates successful people from those who give up at the first sign of trouble. This does not mean we stoically ride into the valley of death. It means we pick ourselves up and try again. Try a different approach, a different tactic. But we keep moving.

One key way to build resilience in trading is to cultivate a growth mindset, as we talked about in the last chapter. Instead of viewing setbacks as failures, see them as opportunities. Consider challenges as chances to improve your skills and strategies rather than seeing them as insurmountable obstacles. I know it is difficult to get back up after the knockdown. It feels good just to lie there and let the feeling of the sting wander away. Shake it off, get back up, and get in the game. By adopting a growth mindset, we can develop a more positive outlook on adversity and approach it with confidence and determination. Maybe not the first setback or second, but there will be a number that we will be able to bounce back in no time.

Another important aspect of building resilience in trading is practicing self-care. Take time to nurture your physical, emotional, and mental well-being through activities like exercise, meditation, and relaxation. By taking care of yourself, you can better cope with stress and setbacks in the market, allowing you to make clearer and more rational decisions. I have a timer set for 30 minutes, and when it goes off, I get up, walk around, and leave what I am doing for a few minutes.

Developing Self-Awareness and Self-Regulation

In his commencement speech named “This is Water”, writer David Foster Wallace told this story:” There are these two young fish swimming along, *and they happen to meet an older fish swimming the other way, who nods at them and says "Morning, boys. How's the water?" And the two young fish swim on for a bit, and then eventually, one of them looks over at the other and goes, "What the hell is water?*

The story's point is that the most obvious, important realities are often the hardest to see and talk about. He spoke about exercising control over how and what you think and being aware of what you pay attention to.

Self-awareness involves taking the time to reflect on our thoughts, feelings, and actions regarding trading. By being honest with ourselves about our strengths and weaknesses, we can better understand how our emotions influence our decision-making process. This awareness allows us to identify any biases or irrational beliefs that may cloud our judgment, enabling us to make more objective and strategic trading decisions. We have them, we all do. The market is not out to get us, even if it really feels that way. I know, I've been there and most likely will visit it again in the future.

Self-regulation is the ability to manage emotions and impulses to stay focused and disciplined when trading. By learning to control emotions such as fear, greed, and impatience, you can avoid making rash decisions that are driven by emotional reactions rather than logic. Developing self-regulation requires practice and patience, but it is a skill that can be honed over time with dedication and mindfulness. Possibly start with a small position size or better yet start by paper trading. As you become more comfortable, gradually increase the size.

Traders who can develop self-awareness and self-regulation are better equipped to handle the ups and downs of the market with more grace and composure. By understanding your emotions and learning to regulate them effectively, you can maintain a clear and focused mindset that allows you to make sound decisions based on logic and analysis rather than emotional reactions. This ability to remain calm and composed in the face of uncertainty can give you a competitive edge in the market and help you achieve greater success in your trading endeavors. While everyone else is running around, we can focus on what is important.

Developing self-awareness and self-regulation are essential components of mastering the psychology of trading. By taking the time to reflect on your emotions and learning to manage them effectively, you can make more informed and rational decisions when it comes to buying and selling assets. With practice and dedication, you can cultivate these skills and develop a mindset that is resilient, disciplined, and focused on long-term success.

Remember, trading is as much a mental game as it is a financial one, and by mastering your emotions, you can unlock your full potential as an investor and trader.

Empathy and Social Awareness in Trading

It's easy to get caught up in the numbers and forget about the human element behind every trade. However, true success in trading requires more than just a sharp mind and quick reflexes - it also requires empathy and social awareness. Understanding the emotions and motivations of other traders can give you a competitive edge in the market, allowing you to anticipate market movements and make more informed decisions. If everyone is bullish, maybe a pullback is nearing.

Empathy is the ability to put yourself in someone else's shoes and understand their perspective. In trading, this means being able to see the market from the point of view of other traders and understanding their fears, hopes, and motivations. By developing empathy, you can better predict market trends and make trades that align with the prevailing sentiment. This can help you avoid costly mistakes and capitalize on opportunities that others may overlook.

Social awareness is closely related to empathy, but it goes one step further by helping you understand the broader social dynamics at play in the market. You can stay ahead of the curve and make more informed decisions by keeping a pulse on the latest news, trends, and developments in the financial world. This can help you identify emerging opportunities and avoid potential pitfalls, giving you a competitive advantage in the market.

Trading is not just about numbers and charts - it's also about people. By developing empathy and social awareness, you can better understand the motivations and emotions driving the market, allowing you to make more profitable trades. So, next time you sit down to analyze the market, remember to consider the human element behind every trade. Your ability to empathize and understand others can be the key to unlocking greater success in your trading journey.

Building Strong Relationships with Traders and Mentors

Building strong relationships with other traders and mentors is important if you are able too. These individuals can provide valuable insights, guidance, and support to help you navigate the market's ups and downs confidently and clearly. By fostering these relationships, you can learn from the experiences of others, gain new perspectives, and expand your knowledge and skills in trading. Should you reach out to a community of like-minded traders, avoid the blowhearts. You will detect them right away.

Traders and mentors can serve as a source of inspiration and motivation during challenging times. They can offer encouragement and advice to help you stay focused and positive, even when faced with setbacks or obstacles. By surrounding yourself with like-minded individuals who share your passion for trading, you can create a supportive network that will help you stay resilient and committed to your goals. Sometimes, people portray trading as a lonely endeavor. It doesn't have to be.

Besides providing emotional support, traders and mentors can also offer practical guidance and expertise. They can help you develop strategies, analyze market trends, and make informed decisions that can lead to profitable outcomes. By learning from those who have more experience and knowledge in trading, you can accelerate your own growth and development as a trader.

Building strong relationships with traders and mentors requires open communication, trust, and mutual respect. It is important to be willing to listen, learn, and collaborate with others in order to benefit from their wisdom and insights. By building a strong foundation of trust and respect with your peers and mentors, you can create a positive and empowering environment that will help you thrive in the world of trading.

Practicing Emotional Detachment and Objectivity

Emotions such as fear, greed, and impatience can cloud judgment and lead to poor decision-making. By mastering the art of emotional detachment, traders can make clear-headed decisions based on logic and reason rather than being swayed by their emotions.

The question becomes, how do we do this? Sometimes, we are required to be cyborgs and just do it. One way to practice emotional detachment is to cultivate a mindset of objectivity. This means viewing the market with a neutral perspective, free from biases and preconceived notions. Hard, I know, but it can be done. By approaching each trade with an open mind and focusing on the facts rather than getting caught up in emotions, traders can make more informed decisions that are based on data and analysis rather than gut feelings.

Another important aspect of emotional detachment is learning to accept losses as a natural part of trading. It's inevitable that traders will experience losses from time to time, and it's important not to let these losses affect your emotional state. By accepting losses as part of the game and learning from them, traders can move on without dwelling on past mistakes and making emotional decisions based on fear of losing again. By the way, it is called “risk taking,” not “sure thing taking." I know it will be difficult to shake off the losses, especially if they have been accumulating. I know the first rule for holes is to stop digging. Don't continue to dig deeper holes.

Practicing mindfulness and self-awareness can also help traders cultivate emotional detachment. By being aware of your thoughts and emotions at the moment, you can recognize when you are being influenced by fear or greed and take steps to counteract these emotions. Mindfulness techniques such as deep breathing, meditation, and visualization can help traders stay grounded and focused on the present moment rather than getting swept up in emotions that can lead to impulsive decision-making.

Leveraging Market Psychology for Profit

"I can calculate the motion of heavenly bodies but not the madness of people." ***Isaac Newton***

Isaac Newton lost significant money during the **South Sea Bubble** in 1720. Initially, he sold his South Sea Company shares at a profit of £7,000. However, caught up in the market frenzy, he reinvested at a much higher price and lost £20,000 (equivalent to over $3 million today). It's a reminder that the stock market can baffle even brilliant minds! By leveraging market psychology to our advantage, we can maximize our profits and minimize our losses.

One key principle of market psychology is to remain disciplined and avoid making impulsive decisions based on emotions. Fear and greed can cloud our judgment and lead us to make irrational choices. By staying calm and rational, we can make informed decisions based on logic and analysis rather than emotion. I know it is hard, but it has to be done.

Another important aspect of market psychology is understanding the concept of herd mentality. In times of uncertainty, investors follow the crowd and make decisions based on what others are doing. However, successful traders know it is often more profitable to go against the crowd and capitalize on opportunities others may have missed.

By mastering market psychology, we can gain a competitive edge in the markets and increase our chances of success. By understanding the emotions that drive market movements, we can expect trends and capitalize on opportunities before others do. This knowledge lets us stay ahead of the curve and regularly make profitable trades.

Understanding our cognitive biases can be a game changer. These biases are the mental shortcuts that our brains take, leading us to make irrational decisions based on emotions rather than facts. One common cognitive bias affecting traders is confirmation bias, where individuals seek information confirming their beliefs while ignoring contradictory evidence. This can lead traders to make decisions based on faulty information, resulting in poor outcomes. By being aware of this bias and actively seeking opposing viewpoints, traders can make more well-rounded decisions that are based on all available information. We have a tendency to discount information we don't want to see.

Another cognitive bias that traders often encounter is overconfidence. This bias can lead traders to take on too much risk or ignore warning signs that their investments may be in trouble. By acknowledging their limitations and seeking feedback from others, traders can avoid falling victim to overconfidence and make more rational decisions.

Loss aversion is another cognitive bias that can affect. Daniel Kahneman and Amos Tversky[27] coined this term in their 1979 paper, which sought to better understand people's decisions under risk and uncertainty. Prospect theory revolutionized our understanding of irrational decision-making by challenging the premise that humans always act rationally and consistently. Loss aversion emerged as a central concept within prospect theory, and it states that people are more afraid of losing than they are of winning. Essentially, the pain of losing something is psychologically stronger than the pleasure of gaining the same thing.

Another important concept is the role of heuristics in decision-making. Heuristics are mental rules of thumb that we use to simplify complex problems. While heuristics can be helpful in certain situations, they can also lead to errors in judgment. By understanding the common heuristics that can affect our trading decisions, we can learn to recognize when they are influencing us and make more rational choices.

Furthermore, understanding the concept of risk tolerance is crucial in trading. Various factors influence our risk tolerance, including our personal experiences, beliefs, and emotions. By assessing our risk tolerance and understanding how it can affect our decision-making process, we can create a trading plan that aligns with our goals and comfort level. Remember, it's important to trade within your means and not let emotions drive you to take unnecessary risks. We will discuss this in greater detail further in the book.

It takes self-awareness, discipline, and a willingness to challenge your own beliefs, but the rewards can be significant. By

[27] Kahneman, D, Tversky, A., '*Prospect Theory: An Analysis of Decision under Risk*' Econometrica, Volume 47, Issue 2 (Mar., 1979), 263-292

committing to identifying and overcoming cognitive biases, traders can set themselves up for long-term success in the world of investing.

Implementing Mental Game Strategies for Trading Success

In trading, it's not just about numbers and charts - it's also about mastering your mental game. As traders, you already know the importance of staying disciplined and focused. But sometimes, our emotions can get the best of us and cloud our judgment. That's why implementing mental game strategies is crucial for maintaining a clear mindset and making sound decisions.

One of the key mental game strategies for trading success is developing a positive attitude toward risk. Instead of viewing risk as something to be feared, see it as an opportunity for growth and learning. By embracing risk and understanding that losses are a natural part of trading, you can approach each trade with confidence and resilience. Remember, every successful trader has experienced losses - it's how you bounce back from them that matters.

Another important mental game strategy is practicing mindfulness and staying present in the moment. Trading can be stressful, especially during volatile market conditions. By focusing on the present moment and letting go of past mistakes or future worries, you can make clearer decisions and avoid impulsive actions. Take a few deep breaths before each trade, and remind yourself to stay grounded and focused on the task at hand.

Visualizing your success can also be a powerful tool. Take a few moments each day to visualize yourself making profitable trades, staying disciplined, and achieving your financial goals. By visualizing success, you can program your mind for positive outcomes and build the confidence needed to make sound trading decisions. Remember, the mind is a powerful tool - use it to your advantage.

Take the time to reflect on your trading psychology journey. We know emotions play a significant role in our decision-making process. We can make more informed and profitable decisions by understanding our emotions and how they affect our trading.

Additionally, we have the opportunity to gain valuable insights into our strengths and weaknesses. By acknowledging our weaknesses, we can work to improve them and become more resilient in the face of market fluctuations. Likewise, recognizing our strengths allows us to leverage them to our advantage and capitalize on opportunities in the market.

Reflecting on our trading psychology journey allows us to identify patterns in our behavior and emotions that may be hindering our success. Are we prone to making impulsive decisions when the market is volatile? Do we let fear or greed dictate our trading strategy? By recognizing these patterns, we can begin to develop strategies to overcome them.

It is important to remember that trading is not just about making money—it is also about personal growth and development. By reflecting on our trading psychology journey, we can see how far we have come and celebrate our successes. Every win, no matter how small, is a step in the right direction towards becoming a more disciplined and successful trader.

Lastly, implementing mental game strategies for trading success also involves seeking support and guidance from mentors and fellow traders. Surround yourself with positive and like-minded individuals who can provide valuable insights and advice. By learning from others and sharing experiences, you can continue to grow and improve as a trader. Remember, success in trading is not just about numbers - it's also about mastering your mindset and emotions. Stay disciplined, stay focused, and implement these mental game strategies for trading success.

Celebrating Your Successes and Learning from Your Failures

Congratulations, fellow traders, it is important to take a moment to celebrate your successes. Whether it be a profitable trade, reaching a new milestone, or overcoming a challenge. Acknowledging your achievements is crucial for maintaining a positive mindset. By celebrating your successes, you are reinforcing the belief in your abilities and boosting your confidence to take on even bigger challenges in the future.

However, it is equally important to learn from your failures. Every trader experiences setbacks and losses at some point in their career. Instead of dwelling on these failures, use them as opportunities for growth and learning. Reflect on what went wrong, identify the mistakes you made, and develop a plan to avoid making the same errors in the future. By learning from your failures, you can turn them into valuable lessons that will ultimately make you a better trader.

Remember, success is not defined by the absence of failures but by how you respond to them. Embrace failure as a natural part of the trading process and use it as motivation to improve and evolve. Adopting a growth mindset can turn setbacks into stepping stones toward success. As the saying goes, "Success is not final, failure is not fatal: It is the courage to continue that counts."

As you celebrate your successes and learn from your failures, remember also to practice gratitude. Take a moment each day to express gratitude for the opportunities you have, the lessons you have learned, and the progress you have made. Gratitude can help shift your focus from what you lack to what you have accomplished, fostering a positive mindset and attracting more success into your life.

Look into the mirror, and what do you see?

Is that you, or is that me?–Wilf Brockmann

Ego is a four-letter word for me. It is a part of us; it just is there in our minds and our subconscious. Our ancestors needed it to survive, and in every sense, today we do, too. Things have changed over time, but the ego still plays a central role in how we operate and function. Our ego enjoys the status quo; it does like change. The ego is that little voice in your mind that tells you everything is ok if you follow this path. Our ego will steer us towards acting in ways that seek approval and admiration from others. It wants respect and seeks it out. Today, our ego acts as a reward and punishment agent through our nervous system. When we expect a positive outcome, we receive rewards as positive neurochemicals, which bring us happiness and joy. If the situation brings a negative experience, we get a shot of negative neurochemicals. These chemicals contribute to our mood swings and will make us nervous, jittery, anxious, fearful, and jumpy.

So, we have to change the narrative and trick the ego. This is a continual challenge, but it needs to be done, and it can be done.

Steven Goldstein has written a book that I recommend. I follow the same mental processes that he outlines, but he explains them in greater detail and much more elegantly than I do. The book titled 'Mastering the Mental Game of Trading.'

Our ego is with us for the ride whether we like it or not, so how can we trick it, subdue it, or convince it to play along? In order to achieve that, we must first understand the cycle we physically and mentally go through when making a trade or a non-trade—or, for that matter, any decision in life that requires some action.

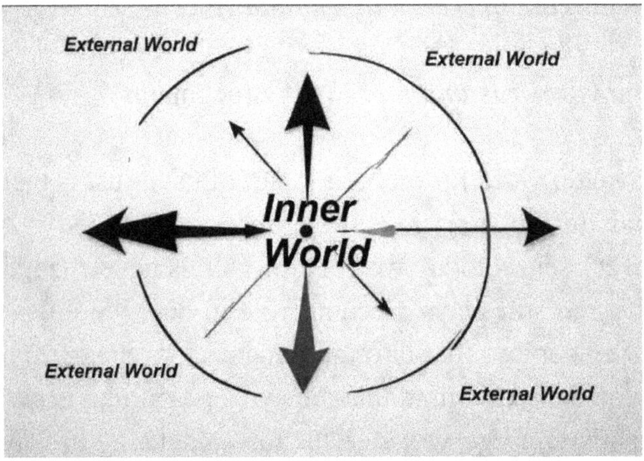

Imagine a circle, if you will. We have two states of existence here. The Inner world represents our thoughts, feelings, and perceptions and is the domain of the ego. The external world is out there, and it interacts with our inner world. The circle edges represent our contact with each of these states. When my sports team wins, I am excited, happy, and euphoric. The circle will expand. The circle contracts onto itself when I am crushed, defeated, and down in the dumps. It doesn't disappear but shrinks. There is a constant battle going on for control of our mental environment. Finding an equilibrium has to be found and can be.

Contact between our inner world and our external world can take place anywhere along the circle. Our other senses play a role in this interchange as well. You may have that one smell of freshly baked apple pie. I know some of you are already salivating. For me, the sound of tires screeching brings me up to high alert, with my back and neck tensing up. You see, in a matter of a year, I was rear-ended three times. The last time I was in the repair shop, I asked them to install a harpoon at the back. I figured if I was going to get hit again, at least they were going to also pay a price.

Decision Cycle

I call it a decision cycle rather than a decision tree because we use it over and over and cycle through it.

In phase one, the start is where everything begins. The start is the foundation upon which we build the rest of our journey. Just like in Star Trek, where the ship must be ready and prepared for the challenges that lie ahead, we, too, must be at our peak readiness to face what is to come. The first phase is about preparing ourselves mentally for exploration and discovery. We are in a neutral state of mind. Our energy levels should be high, our minds sharp, and our mental capital account full. Just like shields on a starship, our mental capital acts as a protective barrier, shielding us from the blows that life may throw our way. Depleting our mental capital makes us more vulnerable to damage and hinders our ability to handle the

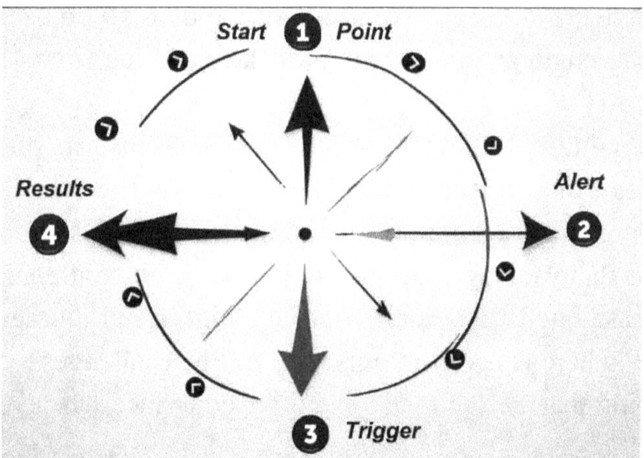

challenges that come our way. Exhaustion, fatigue, and an already state of anxiety are not conducive to this stage. In many cases, we have no choice. We should attempt to start this phase in a state of equilibrium or calm.

During this phase, we are in the exploratory stage, searching our surroundings and gathering information. We are preparing for interaction between our outer and inner worlds, striving to maintain balance and neutrality. We are not acting yet but letting our sensors pick up what is just beyond. Our minds are open and receptive, ready to absorb new knowledge and stimuli that come our way. It is a time of assessment and evaluation as we begin to navigate the depths of our consciousness and explore the uncharted territories within ourselves. Our mental capital is a precious resource, just as important as the financial capital we use in our trading accounts. It is what gives us strength and resilience in the face of adversity.

We must be mindful of how we use this resource, ensuring that we do not deplete it unnecessarily. Just like the crew of the Starship Enterprise, we must be diligent in maintaining and replenishing our mental capital so that we may continue our journey with confidence and purpose. Phase one is the crucial starting point of our journey. It is in phase one where we prepare ourselves for the challenges that lie ahead, ensuring that we are mentally equipped to face whatever comes our way.

In this state, the crew must be ready for anything. We must be ready to spring to our peak readiness, with our mental shields up and our mental capital intact, ready to pounce and react or act. It is a time of exploration, discovery, and self-assessment as we navigate the uncharted territories within ourselves and prepare for the journey ahead. So let us embark on this adventure with courage and determination, knowing that we are well-equipped to face whatever challenges come our way.

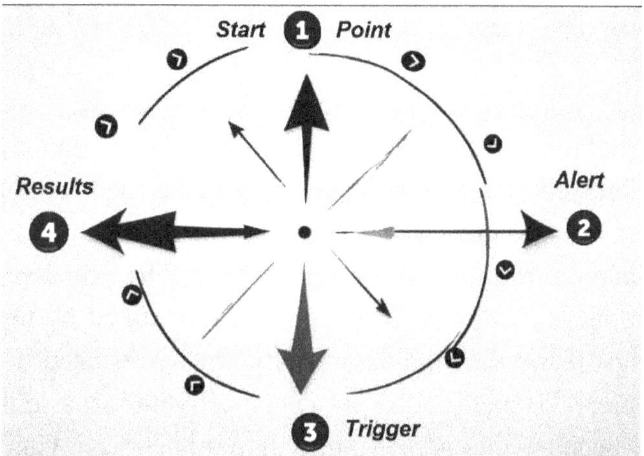

In phase two of our cycle, we are looking for a reason to act, which comes from an alert. Something is happening or about to happen, and we are analyzing if we need to move. We must be prepared to respond rapidly and decisively to any signs of danger or change. I say danger because unless we deem the situation harmless, it isn't. Therefore, we need to start off with a good reserve of energy and be at our peak of readiness, leading us off from phase one. When an alert is tripped, we must be ready to act, whether it is a shift in security rankings, a technical indicator, or a news event. This is not a time for hesitation or doubt. The stakes are too high, and the consequences of inaction could be dire. Let's stay vigilant and prepared, ready to face any challenge that comes our way. We cannot afford to be complacent or passive in our approach to the challenges that lie ahead. You will be amazed at how seemingly mundane and trivial items can spiral out of control and inflict harm and damage.

We must analyze the situation that is presented to us with a clear and focused mind. Is immediate action required, or can we afford to wait and see how things develop? We must make this decision swiftly and with unwavering confidence. As in the analogy in phase one, our Starship and our crew depend on it. The deployment of shields has been ordered, and we are about to call for battle stations. We must be ready to respond with courage and determination. We are still analyzing what the sensors have displayed for us.

A system signal may be about to be triggered, the position may be reaching the selected target, or an event may be on the brink of occurring. Or perhaps the guy driving in front of us has his turn indicator on but is not turning. Will he stop suddenly? Be prepared. If my mental capital is low, I might become very irritated by the driver not turning off his turn indicator. Why am I overreacting? Does it really matter? Try putting this into perspective: the world is not going to end because this person's turn signal is still on. Chill out; you are eating into your emotional capital.

These are not moments to be taken lightly; unfortunately, we do too many times. Each crew member plays a vital role in our mission's success. So let us stand ready, alert, and prepared for whatever may come. Let us face each new obstacle with unwavering resolve and unyielding determination. Our mission is clear, and our purpose is unwavering. Let us go forth and conquer the unknown, one alert at a time. Ok, a little over the top, but pay attention to your surroundings.

Phase Three is a critical point in any decision-making process. It is the moment where we must take action and test true dedication and commitment. However, for many of us, myself included, Phase Three is a vulnerable phase. It is a phase where complacency can easily set in and where we are most at risk of letting our guard down. I have personally experienced the consequences of allowing myself to become lazy during Phase Three.

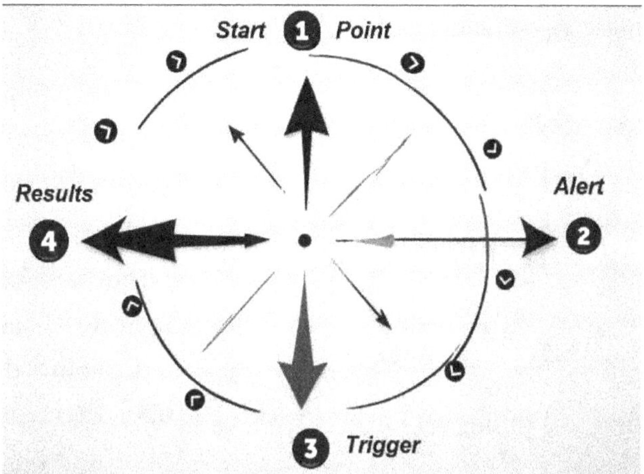

There have been countless instances where I have become too comfortable with how things are going, only to be surprised by unexpected events. During this phase, we should be at our most alert and focused, yet we are often most susceptible to making mistakes. To successfully navigate Phase Three, it is crucial that we stick to the plan and resist the temptation to deviate from it. Go over the checklist, even if you have done it a thousand times before. This is where action is taking place. Moving parts are truly present, it is not a theoretical concept, it is presently unfolding.

Our egos may convince us we can 'wing it,' but this approach is risky and drains us of valuable mental and physical energy. By following this path, we essentially leave ourselves vulnerable with weak or nonexistent shields. Remember that the real action occurs in Phase Three. Our decisions and actions hold the power to create an impact.

Phase Three is the trigger that signals the moment for action. It is a critical phase that requires our utmost attention and focus. With dedication and commitment, we can ensure that we are prepared to face any obstacles that may come our way. Let us not allow complacency to derail our progress, but let us rise to the occasion and seize the opportunities that Phase Three presents. This is our chance to shine, to prove our mettle.

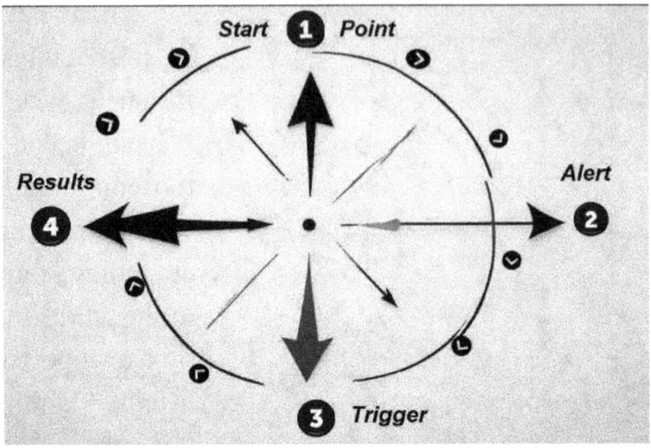

Phase four gives us opportunities to disengage, step back, and reflect, if possible. The action has concluded, and there is nothing else to do. In trading, we are competing against three: the market, your ego, and yourself. Competing against oneself is already challenging enough.

In the realm of decision-making, our actions, or lack thereof, always have consequences. Once we have taken action or chosen not to act in a certain situation, it is crucial that we reflect on the outcomes and learn from any mistakes made. This is where phase four comes into play: we need to analyze our decisions and honestly evaluate what went wrong, what we missed, and how we can correct it. Humility is key during this phase. It takes a strong person to admit when they have made a mistake or overlooked something important.

But in order to grow and improve, we must acknowledge our faults and shortcomings. Only through this process of honest self-reflection can we hone changes in them and avoid repeating the same errors in the future. Letting go is another crucial aspect of phase four. Moving on from past decisions can be difficult, especially if they do not happen as planned. But dwelling on the past will only keep us from progressing and achieving our goals. Just as a soldier must clean their weapon to ensure its effectiveness in battle, we must clean our minds of any lingering doubts or regrets in order to approach the next decision with a clear head.

Our slate has to be cleared with as little residual as possible before entering the decision-making cycle. Mastering the art of letting go is challenging yet essential for success in the ever-changing landscape of decision-making. By shaking off both the good and the bad from the previous cycle, we can approach the starting line with a fresh perspective and a renewed sense of purpose.

We cycle through these stages in the blink of an eye, yet I wanted to slow them down so you could appreciate what we go through in our decision-making process. As we reflect on our past decisions and prepare for the next cycle, it is important to remember that this is all part of the learning process. Each decision teaches us something new about ourselves and the world. By embracing this process with humility and a willingness to learn, we can continue to grow and improve in our personal and professional lives. In phase four of decision-making is a time for reflection, self-evaluation, and preparation for what lies ahead. By honestly assessing our actions, acknowledging our mistakes, and letting go of the past, we can approach future decisions with a sense of clarity and purpose. Through this continual learning and growth process, we can become better decision-makers and better individuals.

We are going to have multiple cycles going simultaneously. Some will be big and important, some small and not that important. Some will take a long time to complete, and some will take a matter of a few moments. Prioritizing cycles is vital. We can deal with many of them quite rapidly and easily. Not all cycles are created equal, and determining which one needs to be triaged is important. What is that old saying, "When you are up to your neck in alligators, it is important to remember your primary task was first to drain the swamp?" Drain the swamp, which may clear up several issues for you by itself.

This is where you need to keep notes in your journal. Every morning, I have a list of items to be reviewed. If something has been sitting on that list and keeps getting moved forward, it's time to deal with it. I treat these as if I were a goalie, and I needed to clear the ball or puck away from the net, or someone would poke it in and score against me.

One item to be vigilant about while we are in this zone is your relationship with your ego. The ego will attempt to wrestle control from you and hijack the situation. Instead of moving forward and cleaning the slate, it will try to proceed straight to the third stage, the trigger, without going through the first two. It will attempt to smooth it down so you think you can handle it and don't need the reset. Believe you do. Before you know it, you are spiraling down for the fall. It will then be that you shake it off and start from square one.

As traders, we sometimes engage in silly behavior. For the longest time, I swore my monitor had been hacked and that somewhere, someone was jerking me around for fun. Every time I entered an order to buy, the security would collapse right afterwards. Yes, I swore at my monitors, hoping to create some guilt by these fathom pranksters.

I suggested the two rules I mentioned before. If I have had three trades in quick succession, either winners or losers, step away and take a break. There will always be another train arriving around the corner. Something is not right, and I don't want my emotions to get involved. Many jurisdictions have a law or practice that calls in drivers for an interview to determine why they should continue holding a driver's license if they have been caught with three tickets in a short time frame. The reason is that if you have had three tickets in quick succession, it is likely that you have committed other infractions that were not detected. They also have statistics that show that the probability of an accident increases sixteenfold. Break the pattern and start fresh later. The other rule I have is once I have closed out a trade or a position, I will erase it from my monitors. I don't want to give my ego the opportunity to point out it should have waited, or I should have sold earlier. Remember, your ego is not your friend, despite what he tells you when it comes to investing or trading.

I picked up the three-time and out rule while playing blackjack. I used to enjoy playing blackjack. I have not played in a couple of years now, but I enjoyed playing because it forced me to obey the rules, be observant, be alert, and keep my emotions in check, all while making some pocket change in the process. Now, we can focus on some other issues regarding emotions. We have talked about these issues before, but they are worth repeating.

We have spoken about these before: fear and greed, two common emotions in trading, can significantly hinder our decision-making process. It's crucial to recognize when these emotions are influencing our actions and take a step back to reassess the situation. It's easy to get caught up in the excitement and adrenaline of the market. We are on top of the world when the trade is working, and we are in the green, yet we will turn depressed when it turns into the red and is underwater. However, it's important to remember that trading is a calculated and strategic endeavor that requires a level head and a disciplined approach. This direct and engaging discussion about fear and greed in trading emphasizes the significance of managing emotions.

A client I coach called me the other day to ask if he should buy more XYZ; he had some extra funds available to him. I questioned the existence of other positions on the buy list that he did not possess. He said yes. I say buy the highest-ranked one you don't own. He said that XYZ is going higher (he had already made 450% in this position by this time.) I insisted it remained a strong buy and would continue to rise, but his greed had caused his portfolio to become imbalanced in a major way. I didn't think he could handle the volatility if it swung lower. I suspect the next 10% drop in the stock, he will call asking if he should sell it down. The fear factor was taking root. He agreed and purchased another highly ranked security that he did not own. At least, that is what he told me.

Just as war can bring chaos and destruction, emotions in trading can lead to financial ruin if not kept in check. *~~War~~ emotions, what are they good for? Absolutely nothing.* By maintaining a clear and rational mindset, sticking to a well-thought-out trading plan, and avoiding impulsive decisions driven by fear or greed, we can navigate the volatile world of trading with confidence and success. So, listen to me when I say: keep your emotions in check and trade wisely.

To truly excel as a trader, one must possess technical skills and knowledge of the markets and conquer the internal psychological challenges that can hinder performance. One of the biggest psychological challenges that traders face is the battle with their emotions. The fear of missing out, the fear of losing money, and the fear of making the wrong decision can all significantly impact trading performance. Emotions can cloud judgment, leading to impulsive decision-making and irrational behavior. To excel as a trader, one must learn how to control these emotions and make decisions based on logic and analysis rather than fear or greed.

Another internal psychological challenge that traders must overcome is self-doubt and self-criticism. The constant pressure to perform can lead to feelings of inadequacy and self-doubt, which can further hinder trading performance. A trader must learn how to silence the inner critic and build confidence in their abilities. Self-belief and a positive mindset are not just beneficial; they are essential for success in trading. Besides conquering internal psychological challenges, traders must also navigate the external challenges presented by the markets.

Market volatility, unexpected news events, and changing economic conditions can all have an impact on trading performance. Adapting to these external challenges and making quick decisions under pressure is essential for success in trading. Mastery of the mental game of trading is the key to achieving exceptional performance and reaching the success you desire. This starts with gaining a deeper understanding of traders' psychological challenges and learning how to overcome them.

Traders can and will succeed by developing emotional intelligence, building confidence, and staying disciplined in the face of adversity. Mastery of the mental game of trading is the key to achieving exceptional performance and reaching the success you desire. By learning how to control emotions, silence self-doubt, and navigate external challenges, traders can excel in the world of trading and reach their full potential, leading to significant financial success.

One of the particularly interesting aspects of trading is that many traders believe the answers lie out there in the market. We seek faster analytics software, better indicators, more knowledge, better insights, deeper analysis, faster news, additional research, the opinions of others, different behaviors, and new skill sets, and yet, all along, the most powerful answers lie within. It is within ourselves where our power and potential lie. We all succumb to the syndrome of being lured by shiny new objects. I will speak about this later on.

Let's create a framework to place our emotions in the right box and control them so that when the unexpected occurs, and it will, we will have an action plan in place to act rather than running around like chickens with our heads cut off.

The Power of Journaling

Despite its many benefits, many people struggle to motivate themselves to journal regularly. It often gets pushed to the back burner with promises of "I'll do it tomorrow." Remember what I taped to my laptop? 'Yesterday, you said tomorrow.' Unfortunately, this procrastination can lead to missed growth and personal development opportunities. When we take the time to journal, we have the chance to look back on our thoughts, emotions, and actions. It is a highly inexpensive form of theory. Walking the dog is a good second. Paper and pen are most effective. I switch from fountain to pen to pencil. The point is that I try to journal every day while the event is happening. Sometimes, I will go back and just scratch my head until I read my notes.

By analyzing our entries, we can identify patterns, behaviors, and habits that may have contributed to both positive and negative experiences. It is truly amazing to go back and read what can be discovered about yourself. This self-reflection can provide valuable insights into our strengths, weaknesses, and areas for improvement. In his famous quote, *"What stands in the way becomes the way." Whatever it is that you find difficult to accept in your mirror is probably your route forward,*" Marcus Aurelius reminds us that the mirror of journaling can reveal uncomfortable truths about ourselves that we may not want to see. However, it is precisely these truths that we need to confront in order to grow and evolve as individuals.

By acknowledging our flaws and weaknesses, we can work towards overcoming them and becoming the best version of ourselves. Journaling allows us to track our progress, set goals, and hold ourselves accountable for our actions. By committing to regular journaling, we can deepen our self-awareness, gain valuable insights, and make positive changes in our lives.

People journal for various reasons. My sister-in-law, Anne, records every time she fills up with gas. She can tell you going back, I figure, maybe 40 years her gas mileage, cost, and so forth. Why? Because she started it and found it interesting. Good for you, Anne, keep on journaling.

So, the next time you find yourself putting off journaling, remember the vast potential it holds for helping you become a better trader - or a better person. Take the time to reflect, identify patterns, and strive for self-improvement. Your future self will thank you for the effort you put in today.

STRESSORS and Stress.

When I first read the article in November 2012 from Advisor One, I focused on the aspect of CNBC as public enemy #1. That goes for all news outlets. They are not our friends; we must remember they are selling us a product, and they get paid by the advertisers. Think about it: some disaster occurs, and for the next week, the various channels fall over themselves, explaining to us that the hang-nail report the President has is critical to national security. I didn't look further into the stress aspect. It didn't occur to me because of my investment process and method. With the program and strategies I had developed and employed, stress over security selection and whether I should stay or go was not a factor. I had developed a rules-based system that was successful and I was sticking to the rules mostly. Not that my life wasn't stressful, far from it.

Here is the article, and I have NOW read the remaining part; I found the rest fascinating.

CNBC: Public Enemy #1?

November 1, 2012

A recent article at *Advisor One* suggests that CNBC is detrimental to the well-being of your clients. In truth, it didn't really single out CNBC. It was applicable to any steady diet of financial news. Here's what the article had to say about financial news and client stress:

Clients get stressed by things you wouldn't predict. This is a classic example, uncovered at the Kansas State University (KSU) Financial Planning Research Center by Dr. Sonya Britt of KSU and Dr. John Grable, now at the University of Georgia, in their recent paper "Financial News and Client Stress." They found that contrary to what you might think, client stress goes up when watching financial news, and hearing that the market went up causes stress levels to rise even higher. "Specifically, 67% of people watching four minutes of CNBC, Bloomberg, Fox Business News, and CNN showed increased stress, while 75% of those who watched a positive-only news video exhibited an increase in stress," they wrote.

Why? "Financial news was found to increase stress levels, particularly among men," wrote Grable and Britt. Surprisingly, positive financial news, like reports of bullishness in the stock market, created the highest levels of stress, they found, suggesting that positive financial news may trigger regret among some people. The authors referred to previous studies of regret that found "people tend to feel most remorseful when they look back at a situation and realize that they failed to take action." The authors' conclusion: Financial advisors should think twice about having office TVs tuned to financial channels.

Surprising, isn't it, to find out that clients were stressed even when the market was going up? The ups and downs of the market appear to elicit client's concerns about their financial decisions. Anything that undermines their confidence is probably not a positive. In fact, one of the important things advisors can do is help clients manage their investment behavior. Financial news appears to work at cross-purposes to that. (Other things do too; the full article has a host of useful thoughts on what stresses clients and how to reduce client stress.)

The relationship between high levels of stress and poor decision-making is well-known to psychologists, researchers, and sports fans around the world. "Our brains operate on different levels, depending on circumstances," Britt told me in an interview. "Under high levels of stress, our intellectual decision-making functions shut down, and our emotional flight or fight response kicks in. " Added Grable: "People will adapt to low levels of stress differently, but overwhelming stress results in predictable behavior. When we are stressed, our brains cannot move to make intellectual decisions.

If we want to help our clients stay calm and stick with their plans, maybe we should ask about their families, their pets, and their hobbies in a relaxed setting rather than inundating them with market data.

I want to help you transition to a more tranquil existence. And no, it does not involve yoga or breathing exercises. They might help, mind you. A stressor is an external environmental stimulus that results in mental worry. Stress involves the feeling of anxiety, real or imagined. It is an individual's emotional response to a stressor. We all overreact to certain situations.

Many years ago, I recall a particular situation when my parents were still alive and still living in town. I was on the phone with a client, and my second line rang. It flashed briefly and then became solid, showing that my assistant had picked it up. It then went dead, indicating that my assistant had taken the message. I continued with my client call, and a few moments later, my assistant opened my office door and came in ash-faced with a look of either panic or extreme worry. I asked the client if I could put him on hold for a moment and then turned to my assistant. She said in a very shaking voice, "That was your mother; she was very upset. I think it is your father." I gathered my wits, thanked her, picked up the phone, and told the client I would call him back. My father had been suffering from Parkinson's for some time now and was requiring more and more help. With a million thoughts racing through my mind, I picked up the phone, took a deep breath, and called my mother. What caused this existential crisis? In a very agitated, frustrated, motherly tone, she spouted out that she had lost the start button on her computer. I exhaled, glanced at my watch, which displayed 11:30, and said I would join them for lunch and then repair her computer. Our minds play these games all the time, and we need to be on guard and not let our imaginations gain control.

We all need some stress in our lives. Without it, we are dead or might as well be. The stock market, being a volatile and unpredictable entity, can cause undue stress and anxiety among investors and traders. The constant fluctuations in stock prices, economic indicators, and global events can all contribute to the stress experienced by individuals involved. Stress from the stock market can have a significant impact on mental health, decision-making abilities, and overall well-being if not addressed adequately.

We view securities in a different light than other assets we may hold. They are usually very liquid, and their prices can and will fluctuate. Some individuals attach extra attributes to them they shouldn't. I view my toaster as a toaster. It stays motionless and performs its designated function: toasting bread. Many people attribute additional qualities to our cars, for example. It gets us around when and where we want to go. Some may see it as a status symbol or a badge of honor. I once owned a BMW 540i, the ultimate driving machine. To be honest, why did I get it? I thought I deserved a gracious gift for myself, and a bit of ego was involved as well. It ended up being quite expensive for me. I had to attend remedial driving school after picking up too many speeding tickets in a very short period.

"Hi, my name is Wilf, and I'm a speeder."

"Hi, Wilf."

Do you know when you're driving along and see an opening up ahead in the other lane? This vehicle would teleport you there; it was that smooth. Did I need the BMW or the Cadillac? No. My favorite car was a Mazda 3. It was a plain Jane vehicle. My son, Benjamin, had leased it and wanted a new car but still had payments left. So, to help him, I turned in the Cadillac and took over his payments. I loved it. The standard was perfect for me; it had no other options. The experience of driving was pure enjoyment, and it didn't respond like a high-strung poodle in the winter, like the BMW. This is what a car was meant to be, for me anyway.

Next, we have securities. Individuals will place their hopes and dreams in them. They hold the key to their retirement, the new house, the children's education, and their philanthropic desires. It may give them bragging rights around the office water cooler or at the family gathering. Ego-driven, in part, for some individuals. They are not the key to your future—you are and the decisions you make with them. They should be your toaster. Use them as they were meant to be used. They are the tools to get you to your goal. You control them to be deployed to the best of your ability. I want to show you how to use your tools effectively as possible. I know you got this.

Understanding how the brain processes stressors is essential to understanding individual responses to stress and how we deal with them. We can divide the brain into three levels, each responsible for different functions: the lowest level controls involuntary bodily functions, the midlevel regulates emotions, and the highest level handles cognitive processes.

We must know how we may respond to stressful situations. Those in high-stress situations may react in a "fight or flight" mode, resisting the opportunity to seek assistance, whether with an advisor or following through with a stated action plan. Measuring an individual's physiological state can give insight into how the brain reacts to stress.

Stress can impair higher-order thinking, causing individuals to focus on immediate concerns rather than long-term goals. Balancing present living and future planning is ideal, but high-stress situations often shift decision-making towards the short-term. This is because stress triggers the fight or flight response, limiting the ability to think rationally about long-term consequences.

When we are stressed, we may exhibit signs such as fatigue, irritability, and poor concentration, which can lead to poor financial decisions. Stress can cause the body to overproduce cortisol, which is associated with negative effects like shortsightedness and depression. As individuals age, cortisol levels tend to rise, affecting decision-making abilities. High cortisol levels can lead to a myopic outlook, focusing decisions in the lower levels of the brain and hindering higher-order thinking.

Managing stress is important for managing our financial affairs and life, as stress can affect memory, decision-making, and overall well-being. We worry about things that are out of our control, the past and the future. We can, however, control how we react to the present. Living in the now is critical. Living in the present while planning for the future is an effective way to manage stress, but this can be challenging for many individuals. Even those who consider themselves long-term-oriented may struggle to make future-oriented decisions when faced with high stress levels, as the fight or flight response dominates decision-making processes.

Understanding how the brain processes stress and the effects of cortisol on decision-making is crucial for making sound financial decisions. By recognizing and managing stress levels, we can help mitigate the negative effects of stress on decision-making and overall financial well-being.

I revisited an intriguing March 2009 study in neuroeconomics. This field has made significant progress in understanding the neurobiological basis of risk in decision-making. It is common to seek advice from experts or others during market downturns.

I found the next part of the study fascinating. In their experiment, the researchers used a functioning MRI to monitor the brain activity of 24 college students while they made decisions concerning swapping a guaranteed payment for a chance at a higher lottery payout. Sometimes, they received written advice from Dr. Charles Noussair, an Emory University economist who also advises the US Federal Reserve. Other times, they decided on their own. To no one's surprise, the students followed Dr. Noussair's advice, even if it was bad or faulty.

The kicker was the brain activity observed. When making decisions independently, without expert advice, activity was shown in their anterior cingulate cortex and dorsolateral prefrontal cortex. These are areas associated with calculating probabilities and making decisions. **Yet when given advice from Dr. Noussair, activity in those areas flatlined.** [28]

When you think about it, the implications are troubling when we take into consideration how unreliable experts are, as noted by Dr. Phillip Tetlock.

That got me thinking about my client calls. I just assumed our decisions were collaborative and that they were paying attention. When I disclosed this discovery to one of my brothers, he confirmed it. He said, "*Whenever you called to talk about making a trade, I turned off my mind because I trusted you. If it was about where we were going for dinner, that's a different story.*"

[28] Engelmann, el at.pp 3.

We saw this type of behavior during the COVID-19 pandemic. The vast majority of the population just went along with what the authorities said without questioning. Many abdicated their freedom and power without a struggle. And still today, I think many are either lazy or lack the motivation to reclaim them.

I listened to an interview given by Dr. Jordan Peterson. In it, he said that when we study Nazi Germany of the 1930s, everyone identifies with Schneider's List or Anne Frank. People never identify with the SS guards. We could never be so evil, yet Dr. Peterson said that a good 35% or more of people during the pandemic would have eagerly handed us to the police for not wearing a mask. We witness countless people who refused to be vaccinated, losing their jobs and being vilified.

Rats, Humans, and Probability

In his book '*Expert Political Judgment: How Good Is It? How Can We Know?*[29]' Dr. Philip Tetlock presented a striking contrast in decision-making. He cited studies in which researchers asked subjects to predict which side of a T-shaped maze would yield food for rats. The maze was designed to place the food randomly, with a 60% chance on one side and a 40% chance on the other. Interestingly, while the rats quickly learned to wait on the side with a higher success rate, human observers rarely saw this pattern. Instead, they made decisions based on new results as they came. This led to a mere 52% accuracy, indicating a misdiagnosis of probability strategies that account for surprise and error. It appears

[29] Tetlock, P. E. '*Expert Political Judgment: How Good Is It? How Can We Know?*', Princeton University Press. 2005

we consistently misinterpret probabilistic strategies that accept the inevitability of randomness and error. This stark contrast between rat and human decision-making underscores the need to recognize our limitations and biases. But don't ask the rats for their thoughts on the direction of the markets.

This finding and others like it have a profound impact on decision-making in politics, economics, and everyday life. The urgency of recognizing and accepting randomness and infallibility is paramount to making informed and successful choices. By acknowledging our limitations and biases, we can strive to enhance our decision-making skills and steer clear of the pitfalls of seeking patterns that are non-existent. Here, the humans over thought and saw patterns that did not exist. We frequently find ourselves in the same situation, highlighting the importance of this insight. As I mentioned previously, we end up seeing patterns that don't exist.

This underscores the intricate nature of the cognitive processes and the challenges we face in accurately assessing situations, especially in a dynamic and volatile environment. The work of Edwards, Estes, Tetlock, and others provides invaluable insights into how people respond to uncertainty and shock, emphasizing the complexity and importance of this aspect of decision-making. Remember, I mentioned that I swore my monitor had been hacked and someone was watching me make trading decisions? Silly, yes, I know, but it sure felt that way.

Dr. Tetlock, whom we discussed at length, has made profound contributions to the fields of decision-making and forecasting. His book, '*Expert Political Judgment*', meticulously dissects the pitfalls of forecasting and the unwarranted confidence that experts often exhibit in their predictions. Dan Gardner also highlighted this in his book 'Future Babble' during our correspondence. I asked him why there was no segment on financial wizards, and here is his response again.

"In my original plan for the book, I had a chapter on financial gurus. Most of it was written, but we dropped it simply to keep the book short, which was necessary, in a practical sense, but also a shame. Some of the money guys I interviewed -- very big names -- were the finest illustrations of the sort of expert we should flee from. But they were confident. Oh lord, were they confident. Absolutely unshakable. No matter what happened, they were right all along. Truly amazing."[30]

Tetlock's research illuminates the importance of acquiring humility and openness in dealing with complex issues, and underscores the necessity of embracing uncertainty and considering multiple perspectives, and leaves the reader with a sense of enlightenment. Many Experts who are paid for their advice fail. Yet, by using insights from experts like Tetlock, we can become more aware of our own biases and blind spots. This knowledge strengthens us and makes us more thoughtful, even when we feel insecure. This is where we must accept humility and abide by my second principal – ***When the facts change, I change my mind. What do you do, Sir?***

On the positive side, the study of possible reasoning and decision-making provides great insight into how we can improve our thinking and problem-solving skills. By adopting a probabilistic approach and accepting uncertainty in a situation, we can make informed and rational choices. This approach encourages flexibility

[30] From the personal correspondence of Wilfred Brockmann dated 30 May 2011

and adaptability, allowing us to handle complex situations more easily.

On the one hand, the negative aspects of this project indicate the existence of challenges and prejudices that influence people's decisions. Our desire to find patterns and make random decisions can lead us astray, ignore important details, or make mistakes. Understanding these limitations is important to reduce their impact and improve decision-making processes. We must always be vigilant about our weaknesses.

We know that rats have a better chance of getting probability right than people. For this reason, we need to employ a systematic investing process. This will remove the pressure and hubbub of the markets, allowing strategies to be researched and probabilities investigated and calculated. A systematic investing process allows us to make decisions based on probability, recognizing that clever decision-making cannot overcome a certain amount of randomness. We wish not to repeat the experience of Long-Term Capital Management personally. As I have said numerous times, it is called risk-taking; otherwise, it would be called sure-thing-taking.

Ironically, humans' inherent sophisticated pattern recognition skills cause us to perceive patterns in probability that are nonexistent. A systematic investment process can reduce or eliminate the "over interpretation" inherent in our own cleverness. Then, we can base our decisions only on the actual probabilities embedded in the data, those decisions will be much better over many trials.

Successful investing is never easy, but a systematic investing process like relative strength, which we use, can eliminate at least one barrier to great performance.

Go further with https://beyondetfspro.com – another shameless promotion.

Harry Markowitz and his personal asset allocation

I would like to highlight some interesting facts regarding risk-taking and the emotions involved in making these decisions. Emotions and most people's fears are much deeper than we suspect. But not yours because you are reading this book, right? I have previously mentioned Harry Markowitz, the Nobel Prize-winning economist who pioneered the field of investment portfolio theory. Walk into any financial institution and tell them you have some money to invest, and they will run you through a series of questions to determine your risk tolerance and design a specific customized portfolio to create your optimum asset allocation. Below is a five-part questionnaire I used in the 90s. Yes, I used this approach for a short time.

1. *"I may need the sums in this account within the next 5 years... YES/NO*

2. *If this account lost money over a year, I would stay with my strategy... YES/NO*

3. *My current personal budget or my other investments cover my current expenses, I will use this account for other... YES/NO*

4. *I am between 45 and 60 years of age... YES/NO*

5. *This account represents less than 25% of my net assets... YES/NO"*

Here is a letter that I sent out during that period.

February 5, 1996

Mr. & Mrs. XXXXX

Dear XXXX

I have enclosed the questionnaire results, which we completed during our meeting on Jan 31, 1996. I use these results in concert with Mercer Investment Consulting Ltd., Canada's leading pension plan consulting firm. Mercer also contributed to the questionnaire, which helps us match your goals and needs with appropriate asset benchmarks. We use the results as a stepping stone to a comfortable portfolio mix and will review the recommendations during our meeting on Feb. 9, 1996.

As I mentioned, asset allocation has the largest single influence on portfolio returns. It is a proven way to provide the **highest possible returns,** given your stated level of risk.

Tactical asset mix recommendations are provided, ongoing, by T.A.L. Investment Counsel Ltd. T.A.L., a Canadian asset allocation pioneer, has successfully used and refined the same fundamental approach to asset allocation since 1973. T.A.L. has grown to become one of Canada's foremost independent portfolio managers, with more than $22 billion in assets under management.

My objective is to understand your needs, which will help to provide you with:

* Sound investment policies (**strategic asset allocation** leading to benchmarks) based on specific goals and needs, as well as historical and projected asset class returns;

* Customized asset mix recommendations (**tactical asset allocation**) based on 12- month projections for major financial markets worldwide

My portfolio management process involves 5 steps.

1. **Establishing** your objectives, needs, and risk tolerance levels.

2. **Matching** your objectives with a long term asset allocation portfolio by Mercer based on long term trends for major financial markets.

3. **Adjusting** your current mix of investments according to T.A.L.'s economic and market forecasts.

4. **Recommending** specific investments based on your current asset allocation.

5. **Delivering** a personalized report outlining your long term strategy, current asset allocation, and current portfolio, as well as any necessary buy-sell decisions

And the letter goes with a recommendation and so on.

So here is the catch. Markowitz created a mathematical model using a set of complicated equations to reduce the emotional bias we have when creating the optimum asset allocation. **Yet, he could not implement his own research, at least when setting up his personal retirement fund.**

"I should have computed the historical co-variances of the asset classes and drawn an efficient frontier." Markowitz later confessed, *"Instead, I visualized my grief if the stock market ... went way down, and I was completely in it.* ***My intention was to minimize my future regret****. So I split my contributions 50/50 between bonds and equities."*[31] (The emphasis are mine)

When faced with an emotional consequence, even the man who invented the efficient frontier became an irrational investor! Honestly, this is just human. Our decisions are often driven by a desire to avoid appearing foolish. This is just what Markowitz did. He felt scared, and we all have this tendency at times. The assumption that investors would ever be rational was simply a faulty premise. To go further into this matter, in my opinion, much of the data being used to fuel these assumptions is faulty. These models use historical data, which by itself is… historical, the past.

Consider the data that would determine how much bond allocation one would have in one's portfolio. Remember my position on bonds in my I Believe segment, I don't. The US Treasury 10-year Note yielded a return of 15.68% in October 1981. The yield reached 0.7% after declining until March 2020. As of July 2024, it yields 4.1%. For the good part of 39 years, we have witnessed a bull market in bonds. I wonder what their models are projecting now for the

[31] Zweig, J., '*How Nobel Prize winners Invest.*' Wall Street Journal, December 26, 1998.

direction of long term interest rates. I suspect whatever figure they use it will be wrong. They are experts, by the way.

Just a side note on interest rates: I predicated the peck on interest rates back then. How, you may ask? Merrill Lynch at the time was underwriting a preferred dividend stock with a yield of 14.75% for CIBC and TransAlta. This gave the security a bond yield equivalent to 22.125%. I called everyone in the country who could fog a mirror and could not sell one share. Even my mother and father turned me down. The typical response was, why should I accept 22.125% when interest rates are going to be 25%. Here, the crowd did not show wisdom.

Therefore, I emphasize a rules-based investment process that you can use to remove emotion from the equation.

In my continued research into the risks, fears, and emotions that investors encounter in making their investment decisions, I came across a paper entitled '*Ambiguity and Nonparticipation: The Role of Regulation*' by David Easley and Maureen O'Hara.[32] They wanted to study whether more regulation injected into the financial infrastructure would increase household participation. Would the participation rate increase if investors knew that strict monitoring of the company's financial statements reduced the likelihood of fraud? We no longer have heady days like those of Jesse Livermore. They said that rates would increase a little, but what really shocked me was the overall participation rate of US families. This study was published in 2009, and I suspected investors were recoiling from the Great Recession.

[32] Easley, D, O'Hara, M, '*Ambiguity and Nonparticipation: The Role of Regulation*' The Society for Financial Studies, Oxford University Press, 2009.

In search of current data, I looked at the US Federal Reserve files and found their report, *'Changes in US Family Finances from 2019 to 2022 Evidence from the Survey of Consumer Finances October 2023.'*[33]

Direct ownership of stocks increased markedly between 2019 and 2022—from 15 percent of families to 21 percent—the largest change on record. *Conditional median stock holdings fell by about half, from $29,000 to $15,000, suggesting new entrants into direct stock ownership held smaller portfolios than longtime stockholding families*[34].

When direct and indirect stock holdings are combined, the 2022 survey showed a step-up in stock ownership to ***58 percent, compared with 53 percent in 2019 and 52 percent in 2016.***[35]

The highlight segment is mine. I never realized that participation in the stock market is so low. It couldn't be because of transaction costs, they are almost zero. It couldn't because of access to a trading platform, it couldn't because of lack of information, it is everywhere. The only thing left is fear, or people will not have the money to invest. We can overcome that hurdle by putting it all together.

Equities will neither make you wealthy nor keep you wealthy. This statement may seem contradictory to what many believe, as investing in the stock market is the only way to grow your

[33] U.S. Federal Reserve Bank, Research & Analysis, *Changes in U.S. Family Finances from 2019 to 2022 Evidence from the Survey of Consumer Finances October 2023*, https://www.federalreserve.gov/publications/files/scf23.pdf, viewed 2 Jun 2024
[34] Fed, pp,16
[35] Fed, pp.17

investments over the long term. However, there is a crucial missing factor in this equation, and that factor is you.

Wealth is not solely determined by the equities but by the actions and decisions made in relation to those investments. Equities alone will not spontaneously grow your wealth without your active involvement and effort. Take charge of your investments, monitor their performance, and make decisions based on market conditions and your financial goals.

Furthermore, simply owning equities is not enough to guarantee long-term wealth. The key to building and maintaining wealth lies in your behavior as an investor. This includes having a disciplined approach to investing, managing your emotions, and staying committed to your long-term financial goals.

One of the most significant challenges investors face is managing their emotions. The stock market can be volatile, and it is easy to panic and make irrational decisions in response to market fluctuations. However, successful investors understand that market volatility is a normal part of investing and remain focused on their long-term investment strategy.

Ultimately, your behavior regarding your investments will determine your success as an investor. Equities are merely a tool that you can use to grow your wealth, but it is up to you to make the most of that opportunity. By being disciplined, managing your emotions, and staying committed to your financial goals, you can behave your way toward wealth. Remember, the equities will not do it alone–you must do the work.

How to blow up your account in a few easy steps.

Blowing up your account, unfortunately, is pretty easy; I know from personal experience. It's easy to fall out of sync with what you're supposed to do. We all break the rules occasionally, but the issue is which rules and when. At least I do, we might become lazy, lose focus, and cut corners. But we must be on guard and not lose our edge. Patience and self-discipline are so critical. Following the rules and establishing a routine is paramount. It's not about following them occasionally; it's about following them every day.

Have you ever strayed from the rules you know you should follow? Maybe you've skipped a workout, procrastinated on a project, or taken shortcuts in your work. It happens to all of us at some point or another. But the danger lies in making a habit of breaking the rules. When we repeatedly cut corners and ignore the guidelines set in place, we set ourselves up for failure. Whether it's in our personal lives or professional endeavors, following the rules is essential for success.

Rules are there for a reason, to maintain order, ensure fairness, and protect us from harm. When we disregard these rules, we not only put ourselves at risk but we also jeopardize the well-being of those around us. Establishing a routine is one of the key ways to stay on track and avoid falling out of sync with what we're supposed to be doing. Following a consistent schedule and routine can better manage our time, stay focused on our goals, and prevent ourselves from succumbing to laziness or distraction. Each step we take towards breaking the rules may seem insignificant, but the cumulative effect can be substantial. Whether it's cutting corners in our work, taking risks with our investments, or neglecting our health, each rule we break puts us one step closer to a potential disaster.

Honestly, nobody wants to ruin their account. Whether it's a financial account, a relationship, or a personal goal, the consequences of breaking the rules can be severe. By staying disciplined, remaining focused, and adhering to the guidelines set in place, we can avoid the pitfalls of straying from the path we know we should be on. So, let's commit to following the rules daily and every moment. Let's establish a routine that keeps us on track and prevents us from falling out of sync with what we should be doing. Agreed?

By staying disciplined, focused, and dedicated to following the rules, we can ensure our success and avoid the pitfalls of breaking them. Let's be vigilant, committed, and on course. It's time to take a stand against falling out of sync and commit to following the rules daily. You got this. We got this. Besides, having a set standard of rules makes life a lot easier. It saves you the time and energy of remembering what you should do next.

1 **Having No Plan** - Having a plan is crucial to success in any aspect of life, especially when managing your accounts. Just as you wouldn't embark on a journey without a map or GPS, you shouldn't try to navigate the treacherous waters of financial management without a solid plan in place. When you get in your car to drive to the store, you have a plan. You consider which route to take, the traffic conditions, the best time to go, and if you need to pick up anything else on the way.

Having a plan ensures you reach your destination swiftly and safely. The same principles apply to managing your accounts. Wishing is not a substitute for a plan. You can't just wish that your finances will improve without taking any action. You need to have a concrete plan with actionable steps and established routines to ensure your financial health.

Just as you have a routine for getting up in the morning, brushing your teeth, and taking a shower, you need one to manage your accounts. This routine should include regular check-ins, updates, and adjustments to ensure that you are on track to meet your financial goals. Without a plan, you are most likely to make hasty decisions based on emotions or impulses, which can lead to financial disaster or turning right instead of left at the intersection.

Having a plan in place gives you a roadmap to follow and helps you make informed decisions about your money. So, what's your routine for managing your accounts? Are you consistent in reviewing your expenses and income? Is there a budget that you consistently adhere to? Do you set financial goals for yourself and track your progress toward achieving them? Don't underestimate the power of having a plan for managing your accounts. It could mean the difference between financial success and failure. Take the time to create a solid plan and stick to it. Your future self will thank you for it. I will discuss my routine and plan in chapter fifteen.

2 Being too arrogant. Being too arrogant in the world of trading can lead to disastrous consequences. When one allows their ego to take control, we think we are invincible and above the herd. This arrogance can blind us to potential risks and market trends that could cause significant losses. Arrogance in trading often comes from a place of overconfidence in one's abilities and knowledge. Finding the perfect equilibrium between confidence and adaptability is crucial.

Remember that no one is infallible. Markets are unpredictable and can swiftly change direction, catching even the most experienced traders off guard. By staying humble and open to new information, traders can better navigate the ever-changing landscape. Arrogance can also lead to risky decision-making and a lack of discipline. Traders who believe they are always right may be more likely to take reckless risks in pursuit of proving their superiority. A more cautious and level-headed approach could prevent significant losses from arising. By acknowledging our limitations and remaining flexible in our trading strategies, we can avoid the pitfalls of arrogance and increase our chances of achieving long-term success.

To succeed in the market, one must have an exceptional level of arrogance that sets you apart from the rest. Arrogance, in this context, is not about being haughty or egotistical. It requires self-confidence and self-belief to defy conventions, trust your instincts, and adhere to your own principles, disregarding others' opinions. It requires courage to be a contrarian and to go against the crowd when they are all following the same path.

It's important to note that in a rising market, it's incredibly easy to confuse good luck with skill. We want to emulate Jess Livermore's behavior. **He always considered himself a market student who occasionally traded correctly**. The market is the great equalizer; everyone is going to get humbled in their journey. It brings us all down to earth at some point. But those who can rise and pick themselves up will elevate above the chaos and noise, having the self-assurance to rely on their own judgment and not be swayed by the whims of the crowd. We are like machines, with emotions stripped out of our decision-making process. We strive to filter out the noise and make clear, rational decisions based on our meticulously crafted action plan. It's a task that is far from simple. Believing that you are right when everyone else tells you that you are wrong requires a certain level of self-confidence. It takes courage to go it alone, to stand apart from the crowd, and follow your own path. We are here along your ride to help.

This self-confidence, self-arrogance, can and will set you apart from the rest and lead you to success in the ever-evolving market world. I have experienced this firsthand in my trading journey. I have had moments where I have taken a different path from my colleagues, where I have gone against the prevailing sentiment and made decisions that others thought were unwise. However, repeatedly, I have discovered that my self-confidence and belief in my judgment have consistently propelled me to success. So, as you navigate the turbulent market waters, remember the significance of self-confidence. Believe in yourself, trust your instincts and your plan, and have the courage to go against the herd. This self-confidence will distinguish you and guide you to success in the unpredictable world of trading. So, embrace your inner contrarian, have the courage to follow your own path, and let your self-confidence guide you to greatness.

My sister-in-law, Lucy, tells a story about fishing one fall afternoon. In the late afternoon, her pole almost ripped out of her hands. She sees this fish arch out of the water, displaying its majestic outline. She had snagged a sturgeon, a fish known for its combative and fierce nature. Struggling for what seemed a lifetime, she manages over time to reel it in. With the help of her husband Tony, he nets the fish and empties it into the bottom of the bottom. Then the fish spits out the hook. It wasn't even hooked. They both stared at the fish with disbelief as its stubbornness and arrogance ultimately led to its demise. They mounted it, and it could be seen in their rec room for many years. We're not saying we are fish, but sometimes we sure do act like that sturgeon. Defiant, stubborn, and arrogant until the very end.

3 **Being afraid to buy a strong stock.** Investing in strong-ranking stocks can be daunting, especially for those new to the game. And yes, even for myself, I get caught up in the moment every

so often before I shake it off and do what is right – buy it. The fear of making a mistake or losing money can often cloud our judgment and prevent us from taking advantage of potentially lucrative opportunities. Studies have shown us that this type of strategy works time after time. However, overcoming this fear and maintaining discipline to buy strongly ranking stocks when the indicators suggest it is crucial and essential.

It may seem counterintuitive—why would anyone be afraid to buy a strong stock? After all, strong stocks are more likely to go up in value and continue going up, right? Even when the numbers are telling us to buy, our emotions can still get the best of us. Your gut instinct, your brother-in-law, and your colleagues—they may all tell you that you are crazy for considering buying that strong stock.

They may point to past failures, market volatility, or a general sense of uncertainty as reasons to stay away. But here's the thing, if you let fear dictate your investment decisions, you may miss out on some of the best opportunities in the market. Take it from someone who has been there—I remember the emotional struggle I went through when I was considering buying Constellation Software. It was a strong-ranking stock with a clear buy signal, but I was hesitant. It was sitting at $170, up from the mid-$60 range the year before. I was scared of making the wrong decision, of losing money, of being judged by others. In the end, I took a leap of faith and hit the buy button. And you know what? It turned out to be one of the best decisions I ever made. The stock went up and up and up, and we made a handsome profit. More importantly, I learned a valuable lesson about the importance of discipline in investing, and so did my clients. Trust the signals.

Now, when I see a buy signal, I act without hesitation. I have trained myself to listen to the indicators, which are soulless and impartial. They don't care about my emotions or fears—they only care about the numbers, and the numbers are telling me to buy. So, I urge you to do the same. Trust in the indicators, trust in the data, and, most importantly, trust in yourself. Don't let fear hold you back from buying strong stocks. Have the discipline to make those tough decisions, even when everyone around you tells you not to.

Remember, fortune favors the bold. Take a chance, trust in the numbers, and watch your investments soar. Don't let fear stand in the way of your success. Be brave, be bold, and be unafraid to buy those strong stocks. Your portfolio will thank you for it.

5 **Selling a strong stock because it is up.** Investing in the stock market can be a rollercoaster of emotions. When we see our investments rise in value, it can be tempting to cash out and take our profits before the market can turn against us. However, selling a strong stock simply because it is up is not wise.

Many financial experts recommend that investors sell some of their more profitable positions and use the proceeds to balance their portfolio by investing in the losing positions. Think about it: why would we want to cut short the things that are working well in order to buy more of the stuff that is not? It just doesn't make sense. Instead, I propose a different approach: sell the positions that are not performing well and reinvest that money into the positions that are actually working.

This strategy not only makes more logical sense but can also lead to higher returns in the long run. The advisors who push the idea of 'balancing the portfolio' by selling winners and buying losers may argue that the winning positions could fall soon. While this may be true in some cases, it is also possible that those winning positions could continue to grow and provide even higher returns. You could be missing out on significant gains by selling off those positions prematurely.

Furthermore, why would we want to invest more money into already underperforming positions? This increases our risk exposure and decreases our chances of making a profit. Instead, it makes much more sense to cut our losses and reallocate that capital into positions that have the potential to grow.

I urged you not to follow advisors' advice on selling winners and buying losers to 'balance the portfolio.' Instead, consider a more strategic approach of selling underperforming positions and reinvesting that capital into flourishing positions. This way, you can maximize your returns and potentially achieve greater investment success. Let us not settle for mediocrity when we can strive for excellence.

We purchased stocks because it gave us a buy signal. That is half of the equation. We are looking for a signal to buy, and when we receive that signal, we make our move. However, many investors cannot realize that selling a stock is just as important as buying it. The sell signal is an essential part of the equation. It allows us to lock in our profits and prevent potential losses. We want the market to tell us to sell, not our emotions or our advisors. By waiting for a sell signal, we ensure we make a rational decision based on market conditions rather than emotions. It can be tempting to sell a stock simply because it is up and profitable. However, cutting our profits short can prevent us from maximizing our gains. By waiting for a sell signal, we are truly giving ourselves the opportunity to benefit from our investment.

So next time you feel tempted to sell a strong stock simply because it is up, remember to wait for the sell signal. Have confidence in your initial buying decision and let your investment reach its full potential. Don't let impatience and greed cloud your judgment. Wait for the sell signal and rationalize based on market conditions. Your portfolio will thank you in the long run. I will go into greater detail and explain the process we use in our app, beyondeftspro. Also, the only people I know that can buy at the bottom and sell at the top are liars. I have positions I would never have dreamed would perform so well. They are like the Eveready Battery Company's Energizer Bunny. They just keep going and going and going. You need more Eveready Energizer Bunnies in your account.

5 **Holding on to a losing position in the hopes it will come back.** It's a common pitfall for many traders and investors to cling to a losing position, hoping it will rebound. However, this approach is a perilous game, often leading to substantial financial losses and emotional strain. In the realm of investing, decisions should never be driven by hope alone. It is essential to ground them in meticulous analysis and evaluation of risks and system signals. By holding on to a losing position, we will assume you have gotten a signal and then let it lapse. That is okay; sell it now. Do it.

One of the main reasons people hold on to losing positions is because of arrogance, which we just spoke about. We know our position will eventually turn around, right? This is a risky mindset, as the market is unpredictable and can shift abruptly. Steering the river of the market is a futile effort and can cause disastrous consequences. Another reason for holding on to losing positions is failing to accept the sell signal. Listening and cutting your losses is important when the market tells you to sell. Each of our three guiding principles embodies the concept of cutting losses.

They are, again, "*Prices are never too high to begin buying and never too low to begin selling.*" Then, "*When the facts change, I change my mind. What do you do, sir?*" And finally, *"A man should look at what is, and not what he thinks should be.;*

Ignoring sell signals can lead to further losses and prolong the pain of losing a position. It is important to have a disciplined approach to trading and investing and to follow your trading plan without hesitation. When you continue to hold on to a losing position, it can become a source of anxiety and stress. Every month, when you receive your statement, that losing position will be the first thing you see. It will weigh heavily on your mind and cloud your judgment. It's important to know when to exit a trade that isn't going in your favor to avoid further losses.

I explained my selling process to clients by saying that getting a sell signal is the same as getting a report from your doctor that you have cancer. You will not tell him you will think about it and get back to him. I want to cut it out right now without delay before it spreads. Don't let a losing position continue to haunt you. Cut your losses and move on. Your account will thank you for it.

6 **Trying to bottom-fish a stock in a downtrend** Trying to bottoming-fish a stock in a downtrend can be risky. It is important to remember that the trend is your friend, and if a position is trending downward, the trend is down for a reason. I don't know why it is falling. All I know is that the market is signaling a downward trend, and the probability is that this trend will continue. I don't need to pick the bottom or sell at the top. I am not greedy, I just want the middle meaty part of the upward trend. Bottom fishing is the act of trying to buy a stock at its lowest point, hoping it will reverse and turn upwards. This is like adding to a losing position and averaging down, both of which can and are dangerous strategies. Trying to

bottom fish stock makes it easy to fall into the trap of thinking that the stock is a bargain and will surely turn around in your favor. Don't try to steer the river.

This simply relies on a hunch and lacks any valid signals or data. Instead of relying on emotions and gut feelings, it is important to trade based on concrete signals and indicators. Deciding based on emotions can cloud your judgment and lead to poor trading choices. Instead of trying to pick the bottom, it is better to follow the trend and trade based on valid signals. Remember, the trend is your friend, and it is always better to trade smart than based on hunches and emotions. There will always be opportunities for those who practice patience and discipline. They look so tempting, but trust me, it is for the best, (he says in a fatherly tone.)

7. **Buying a stock because it is a good value or a good company**. Daily, investors are faced with the decision of buying a stock because they believe it to be a good value or a good company. However, value is a subjective term that can vary depending on who you ask. Some investors may look at a company's financial statements and see value in a stock that is trading at a discount, while others may see value in a company's growth potential and future earnings.

However, the problem with buying a stock solely based on its value is that it may take years for the investment thesis to play out. Remember, I spoke about the bank's chief strategist mentioning value investors should be willing to wait up to 10 years for a play to work out? This is not a feasible strategy. Furthermore, the dot com bubble serves as a cautionary tale for investors who emphasize a company's perceived value too much. Many companies were considered valuable during the dot com era, only to go bankrupt when the bubble burst.

This highlights the importance of not relying solely on a company's balance sheet to determine its value. Supply and demand dynamics will ultimately determine the price of a stock. For me, the true value of a stock is determined by the capital appreciation potential and not a series of numbers on a balance sheet. Balance sheets can be fudged and tampered with, as we have seen from the Enron experience.

We all know that investing can be daunting for those with experience and, more so, for those new to the game. The consideration of a stock being a good value or a good company may tempt people to buy it. However, when it comes to investing, the ultimate goal is to make money, and in order to do that, one must carefully analyze the potential growth of a stock. We want the market to tell us what is of value and when. Supply and demand will aid us in that endeavor. It is difficult to manipulate the price of Apple or Exxon Mobil. Walmart, McDonald's, and Home Depot might be good companies, but why would I want to be a holder if the stock just sits there? I want to hold positions that make me money, not make me feel good.

8 **Falling in love with a position**. Stop it. As traders, we have a responsibility to ourselves and our clients to make sound and rational decisions when it comes to allocating our capital. We cannot afford to get caught up in the hype surrounding a particular position, no matter how enticing it may seem. It's easy to fall in love with a stock that promises to break the internet or cure cancer, but until it actually delivers on those promises, it's just another position in our portfolio.

We have a limited amount of capital to work with, and we need to ensure that we are making the most of every penny. Holding on to a position just because we have been told it is the next big thing is not a smart investment strategy. If the position does not look strong technically, if it is not performing as we had hoped, then it is time to let it go. Getting caught up in the story surrounding a particular position can be tempting. We may hear rumors of breakthrough technology, unprecedented growth potential, or revolutionary new products. But if the numbers don't add up, if the technical indicators are not in our favor, then we need to be disciplined enough to move on.

We cannot afford to let emotions cloud our judgment in trading. Falling in love with a position can lead to irrational decision-making and costly mistakes. We need to approach each trade with a clear head and a healthy dose of skepticism. If a position is not performing as expected, if it is not meeting our criteria for success, then it is time to cut our losses and move on to the next opportunity. Don't fall for the hype around a specific stance. Do not allow yourself to be seduced by the hype surrounding a particular position. Stick to your trading plan, trust your instincts, and do not be afraid to let go of a position that is not living up to expectations. Remember, our goal as traders is not to fall in love with a position but to make smart, calculated decisions that will yield the best possible return on our investment.

9 **The Search for Perfection.** The quest for perfection is a noble pursuit that drives us to achieve greatness. However, the notion of perfection can often lead us down a rabbit hole of never-ending dissatisfaction and disappointment. One factor that plays a significant role in this search for perfection is our constant desire for 'shiny new objects. 'I go into further detail in chapter 15. Advertisements and promotions constantly bombard us, promising the next best thing - a new trading system that will revolutionize our success, a new gadget that will make our lives easier, or a new diet that will finally help us achieve the perfect body.

We are seduced because these new tools promise to help us finally reach the pinnacle of success and happiness. However, constantly chasing after the latest and greatest can actually hinder our progress towards true excellence. Instead of focusing on mastering one skill or system, we spread ourselves thin by jumping from one shiny object to the next. This scattered approach leaves us good at nothing and mediocre at everything. In order to truly excel and achieve perfection, we must learn to stay focused and committed to our goals. As the Dalai Lama wisely said, *"If you walk, walk. If you sit, sit. Whatever you do, don't waddle."*

We must have the strength, courage, and conviction to stick to a plan and see it through to the end. Perfection is not about constantly seeking something better but about honing our skills and continuously improving ourselves. It is about learning from our mistakes and failures and using them as stepping stones towards greater success. So, let us resist the temptation of shiny new objects and instead focus on what truly matters – hard work, dedication, and a relentless pursuit of excellence. Only then can we truly achieve perfection.

For myself, the Brockmann Method, embodied in the app Beyond ETFs pro, provides me with the comfort of knowing that I don't need that new system with all its bells, flashing lights, and whistles. The grass is not always greener on the other side. My approach is adaptive, and I liken it to a heat-seeking missile always searching for the strongest security in the universe of my choosing and guiding me to avoid the securities that are, now, the losers. Things change in the markets, and so do the rankings.

"Never risk what you have and need for what we don't have and don't need."

— Warren Buffett

12. Risk Management

Risk control is the best route to loss avoidance. Risk avoidance, on the other hand, is likely to lead to return avoidance as well." - Howard Marks

This quote from Howard is so true. I have it taped on another of my monitors. How can we implement risk controls? For starters, by following the rules you set up. If it says to sell, then sell. If it says to avoid, you avoid despite what the talking head on TV said. It is an integral component of the plan.

Risk control is a fundamental aspect of managing investments and minimizing potential losses. Howard Marks, a renowned investor, author, and co-founder of Oaktree Capital Management, has emphasized the significance of risk control in the world of finance. In his statement, Marks emphasizes the significance of striking a balance between risk-taking and risk management in order to attain optimal outcomes in investment strategies. That is what we want. These are factors you need if you are managing a few hundred dollars to a few million. The processes and steps are the same. Mind you, with a few million, there might be some additional safeguards, but the rules are basically the same.

The concept of risk management has evolved over centuries, with individuals and institutions developing strategies to protect assets and optimize returns. In the early days of commerce, traders faced the risk of losing their investments due to unpredictable market conditions, natural disasters, or political turmoil. To mitigate these risks, traders often diversified their portfolios, conducted thorough research, and implemented hedging strategies to protect their assets. Remember what I have said about over-diversifying, or as I also like to say, "di-worse-ifying."

The Chinese merchants, who devised the concept of marine insurance to protect their goods during sea voyages, can be credited with one of the earliest forms of risk management. The practice of pooling resources to cover potential losses laid the foundation for modern insurance and risk management practices. As trade networks expanded and economies became more interconnected, the need for sophisticated risk management tools grew exponentially.

In the 17th century, the Dutch East India Company pioneered the issuance of shares and bonds to finance their expeditions, effectively spreading risk among investors and reducing the exposure of any single individual to potential losses. This innovative approach not only changed the way capital was raised but also introduced the concept of risk-sharing in the investment community.

The Industrial Revolution of the 18th and 19th centuries brought about significant advancements in technology, transportation, and manufacturing, leading to increased economic prosperity and investment opportunities. However, with the growth of industries came unknown risks, such as supply chain disruptions, labor strikes, and market fluctuations. To counter these risks, corporations adopted more sophisticated risk management practices, such as forward contracts, commodity futures, and options trading.

The 20th century saw the rise of modern portfolio theory, spearheaded by Harry Markowitz, a renowned economist who introduced the concept of diversification and asset allocation to optimize risk-adjusted returns. Markowitz's work laid the foundation for modern risk management practices, emphasizing the importance of balancing risk and return to achieve optimal investment outcomes. His groundbreaking research paved the way for the development of quantitative models, such as the Capital Asset Pricing Model (CAPM) and the Black-Scholes model, which are used extensively by investors and financial institutions to assess and manage risk.

I wanted to mention Markowitz's and CAPM in particular since I do not agree with them. I recall, while taking my MBA, driving for 8 hours in order not to miss this one particular class to scream my objection to these theories. For six of those 8 hours, I rehearsed a rebuttal that I was sure would land me a teaching position for my clever wit, charm, intellect, and good looks. As I lobbed my first soft volley to the professor, waiting for him to respond so I could perform my surgical attack, he responded, "That is fine; we just use these as starting points to move on." This left me speechless, and hence, no teaching position.

The failure of banks and financial institutions in the aftermath of the 2008 financial crisis exposed the shortcomings of conventional risk models, leading to the scrutiny of risk management practices. As an experienced investor with decades of experience in the financial markets, Marks emphasized the importance of risk control in navigating volatile market conditions and minimizing potential losses. In his book, "The Most Important Thing: Uncommon Sense for the Thoughtful Investor," Marks argues that risk management should be the cornerstone of any investment strategy, as it determines an investment portfolio's long-term viability and success, to which I agree. To see how we implement our protocols, visit https://beyondetfspro.com

This philosophy on risk control resonates with me and many other investors and financial professionals who recognize the importance of preserving capital and managing downside risk. By focusing on risk control rather than risk avoidance, investors can construct resilient portfolios that can withstand market fluctuations and economic uncertainties. We wish to emphasize maintaining a margin of safety, conducting thorough due diligence, and sticking to disciplined investment guidelines.

Technology advances, data analytics, and artificial intelligence are reshaping the identification, measurement, and mitigation of risks, leading to significant transformations in the field of risk management. Machine learning algorithms, predictive modeling techniques, and risk assessment tools are revolutionizing how investors and financial institutions assess and manage risks in real time. Integrating big data and predictive analytics into risk management processes will enable investors to make more informed decisions, anticipate market trends, and navigate complex risk landscapes with greater precision.

Risk control is the best route to loss avoidance, as Howard Marks stated precisely. By adopting a proactive approach to managing risks, investors can protect their capital, preserve their wealth, and achieve long-term financial success. Risk avoidance can lead to return avoidance, as investors may miss out on profitable opportunities by shying away from calculated risks. A balanced and well-diversified portfolio, combined with robust risk management practices, can help investors navigate volatile market conditions, capitalize on emerging trends, and achieve their investment objectives. By learning from the lessons of the past, leveraging the insights of influential figures in risk management, and embracing innovative technologies, investors can position themselves for success in an increasingly unpredictable and competitive financial landscape.

I was explaining to my son and daughter one weekend when they both had come home for a visit to the wonders and marvels of an Iron Condor option trade right before a company's earnings announcement. With excitement, I explained how the option premiums were high and how, by placing a put and call credit spread just outside the expected volatility range, one could pick up a nice return for a few days of holding the position. I outlined the premium would collapse should the stock stay within the band placed by the put and the call spread. Also, the risk control parameters should be put in place should the stock trade through the established bands. When I had stopped, they both were silent, then turned to look at each other for a moment, when once again, turning to me, and just continued to stare in silence. After a few more moments finally, Benjamin spoke up and said, 'Dad, you're going to jail." I made a note to myself to work on my presentation skills a little more.

"There are risks and costs to a program of action. But they are far less than the long-term risks and costs of comfortable inaction – John. F. Kennedy

With the ever-changing global economy, investors face unique challenges and opportunities that require careful consideration and analysis. Doing anything in the investment world has its own costs and risks. However, the consequences of inaction and complacency can be worse in the long run. One key principle that guides investing should be the idea that taking action has costs and risks, but these are often far less than the long-range risks and costs of remaining stagnant or inactivity. Some situations call for action, while others require inaction. The critical part is determining when. If I have a toothache, I better have it looked after, or it will worsen. The same is true with one's portfolio. By the way, I have never had a tooth heal on its own.

Kennedy's quote encapsulates the idea that taking proactive steps and engaging in strategic decision-making may involve some short-term sacrifices or risks. Still, in the long run, the benefits outweigh the costs of complacency. We see this in our daily lives. It is always wise to act now rather than wait for the perfect time or for that stock to return in line. I have a quote taped to my laptop taken from a Nike ad, "*Yesterday, you said tomorrow*." Look after that toothache before it becomes worse.

In the realm of investing, this quote encourages investors to step out of their comfort zones and embrace a more proactive approach to managing their portfolios. It urges investors to consider the risks and costs associated with remaining passive and not adapting to changing market conditions. By taking action and making informed decisions, investors can position themselves for greater financial success and stability in the long term, offering a beacon of hope and optimism in an ever-changing market.

Throughout history, many instances in the world of investing have exemplified this principle. One such example is the Great Depression of the 1930s, where failure to take decisive action and implement effective policies led to a prolonged economic downturn. In contrast, during times of economic crisis, individuals and institutions that took proactive measures and invested in opportunities that others may have overlooked could thrive and recover more quickly. During the 1929 market crash, Jess Livermore made a fortune while Benjamin Graham lost everything he had. (Graham is the other half of the famous Graham and Dodd, the fathers of modern fundamental analysis)

In more recent times, the global financial crisis of 2008 serves as another poignant example of the costs and risks of not taking action. Many investors and financial institutions remained passive and failed to anticipate or respond effectively to the unfolding crisis. I am a perfect example of not taking action. My lack of action in the face of continued red flags cost me and my clients dearly. As a result, they suffered significant losses and faced long-lasting consequences. Those who took decisive action adjusted their investment strategies and seized opportunities to capitalize on market fluctuations could weather the storm and emerge stronger.

The concept of "failing to act" can have detrimental effects on investment portfolios. In today's fast-paced and interconnected world, where financial markets are constantly evolving, and new opportunities arise, remaining idle can lead to missed chances for growth and potential disadvantages compared to those who embrace change and take calculated risks.

One key aspect of this principle is the importance of being proactive and forward-thinking when investing. Instead of reacting to market trends or events, successful investors anticipate changes and position themselves accordingly. By adopting a proactive approach, investors can minimize the risks and costs associated with inaction and capitalize on opportunities that may not be readily apparent. We all experience procrastination and inertia at times.

A small amount of risk is essential for all of us.

The paradox of risk in investments is intriguing. We're often fixated on the idea of safety, drawn to it like moths to a flame. Yet everything we do involves some level of risk. Even a safe government bond investment carries some risk, as I explained in the I Believe section.

Consider risk as matter, it is neither created nor destroyed but always present. When you invest in something perceived as safe, like a US Treasury bill, you're not eliminating your risk; you're merely swapping the risk of losing your money for the risk of losing purchasing power through inflation. The risk hasn't disappeared; you've just exchanged one form of risk for another. This concept of risk substitution is a key aspect of investing that needs to be grasped.

Business report

BRIEFLY

Are they going to stop the crash?

Investors switch to gold

Panic sweeps markets around world

How local companies did

DOW YSE GOLD

DOLLAR

Ripple effect will soak everyone, economists say

'Too early to tell' what impact will be

We have witnessed this overreliance and the placebo effect of thinking everything is safe. I harken back to the 1987 market crash. That was one hell of an event. I remember it vividly, as though it happened just yesterday. Things looked a little suspect during that summer when everyone waited around the Dow Jones News Ticker for the Fed M1 figures each month to be reported. After each release, the market would sputter and yaw. The distance from top to bottom of the yaw widened out. We all had faith in portfolio insurance that was supposed to protect us against any catastrophic decline.

The market closed sharply lower on Friday, and we all left for the weekend knowing we were whistling past the graveyard. Monday started off as a bloodbath, and it continued the entire day. Nowhere offered refuge, and nowhere allowed escape. The best phone call of the day was at 4:30 from my son, Benjamin, who was in grade one. His cartoon program had been halted to announce the market's decline. He called to let me know that he had some money in his piggy bank and that if I needed it, I could have it. I asked him a couple of years ago if that offer was still open, and he told me no.

Ken Wightman/London Free Press

It's a mess

A harried Wilfred Brockmann, broker with Merrill Lynch in London, has a busy day Monday consulting with clients as he and the rest of the world watch the bottom fall out of stock markets in North America and overseas.

Panic sweeps markets around world

The truth about that picture of me[36] is that the photographer was on my right side, and I could hear the camera clicking as he took photos. In the one before this one, I was scratching my nose with my left hand, and I thought it would look like I was picking my nose. On the worst day in market history!! So, I leaned back,

[36] Wrightman, K. *London Free Press*, October 20, 1987, Business Section pg.1

and that is the picture they published. Many newspapers across the country published the picture that was circulated by the wire services. When people would call and say they saw the picture, I would tell them it was when I talked to them. I'm a salesman, remember?

Investors and people are way too risk-averse. We get snookered in deals that are supposed to be "low risk," primarily because their risk aversion leads them to lunge at anything pretending to be safe. Psychologists have documented that individuals make more errors from being too conservative than too aggressive. Investors make that same mistake. For example, nothing is more revered than a steady-Eddie fund. Investors scour magazines and databases to find a fund that (paradoxically) is safe and has a big return. (News flash: if such a stock existed, you wouldn't have to look hard.)

Funds that post big returns in good years but also lose a lot of money in down years **tend to do better over time than funds that post slow, steady returns without ever losing** much. Contrary to popular belief, investments with higher volatility can often outperform those with steadier returns, especially over the long term. A decade-long comparison of volatile and less volatile funds revealed a clear trend- those with significant performance swings emerged as the winners, making roughly twice as much money. These are the strategies we employ at BAT-Brockmann Analytics & Trading and hpps://beyondetfspro.com. (Shameless plug) This underscores the potential benefits of embracing volatility in our investment strategies rather than shying away from it because of risk aversion. Therefore, we have specific rules for getting out of a trade. Before even getting into a trade, we establish specific rules. They are not, *"We will wait until we break even"* or *"Just a little higher."*

This is a game-changer. While risk aversion may be suitable for some investors, it's time to reconsider if it's hindering your long-term returns. After all, enduring a less pleasant experience like eating Alpo might be worth it if it leads to higher returns. We should also consider returns instead of fixating solely on volatility.

When you talk, you are only repeating what you already know, But when you listen, you may learn something new. — Dalai Lama

This also applies to the markets. In fact, I would argue that listening (and reflecting on market action) is all relative strength is really doing.

13. Operating System

I was purchasing a new laptop computer years ago. I needed a smaller, lighter laptop for my winter in Mexico City. Walking is challenging in the North with all the winter snow, ice, and cold, but I still love it. I love Mexico City as it is green, vibrant, and a heck of a lot warmer. Mind you, Cancun would be better, but then I would sit around all day and not move. So I need a laptop in my backpack as I walk the green spaces in Mexico City, stop at my favorite cafes along the way, and check up on the markets. I had an apartment in the La Condesa area, a truly beautiful area. It was conveniently close to Universidad La Salle, where I attended years later to enhance my Spanish skills.

Before leaving, I talked about investing and the market with a neighbor. He was having difficulty understanding what I did and how I did it. I explained to him that to be successful in investing, one requires an operating system like the one on every computer. This operating system facilitates you to read and run all the software programs seamlessly. Operating systems provide a set of instructions and rules that tell the computer how to run. Without an operating system, the software cannot run. Investing successfully works in the same way. Investors must have an operating system and rules deeply entrenched in mind to work from before they can become successful with any investment process.

This operating system is the core belief the investor grasps and wholeheartedly embraces. It's like getting religion on Wall Street. At some point, all successful investors must find some church on Wall Street that they can believe in and stick to. I am a financial evangelist, called to save investors from themselves and their advisors.

Many investors devoutly subscribe to the church of fundamental analysis in their approach to investing. This method only delves into the internal qualities and characteristics of the underlying company. It does not consider timing, entry and exit points and above all, supply and demand imbalances.

Across the street is the church of Technical Analysis. Supply and demand imbalances are nothing more than investor sentiment. Other sects of this church might involve astrology, Elliot Wave, Fibonacci retracement numbers, Gann angles & waves, cycles, seasonality, candlestick charts, bar charts, or other methods you will embrace.

Believe me, I've attended these services. I have only found the church of Relative Strength wanting on Wall Street. Its approach is straightforward and lenient. It adapts and includes all markets and securities. The fundamental premises of Relative Strength are true to the markets and evident outside the confines of Wall Street, and one can find them in everyday life.

At BAT-Brockmann Analytics and Trading, we subscribe only to one irrefutable method. Economics 101 - the Law of Supply and Demand. If you want to go back to the basics, with a methodology that has stood the test of time going back over 100 years, in bull and bear markets and one that is easy enough to learn whether you are age 8 or 80, then you are reading the right book. This operating system will carry you through your investment endeavors, from stocks, ETFs, and mutual funds to commodities and beyond.

Point-and-Figure

As investors, most of us have difficulty coping with the rapid-fire stream of data presented to us in today's market. It is similar to drinking from a fire hose. It comes at us so fast. Thinking logically and navigating the complex decision-making process is challenging. The problem is not that we have too much information. The problem is managing and processing this information. What is important and what is not? The question is how to control that massive information flow and break it down into understandable bits that we can use to make effective decisions. We have decision overload.

Charles Dow, the first editor of The Wall Street Journal, was instrumental in organizing data in a meaningful matter in the 1900s. He was the first person to record stock price movement and developed a method of analysis called Figuring, which eventually led to the point-and-figure method, or PnF for short. The Point-and-figure method of recording stock prices is another way to organize data. We are all familiar with the traditional line chart. These charts track the price and the time across an X and Y axis. What is unique about PnF is that it tracks only the price. It leaves out time.

At the turn of the twentieth century, some astute investors noticed that many of Dow's chart patterns had a tendency to repeat themselves. During that time, there were few regulations and no Securities and Exchange Commission. Stock pools dominated the action, and outsiders arrived very late for the party. It was essentially an exclusive club of insiders. The Point-and-figure charting method emerged as a logical, organized way for traders to record the supply and demand imbalance. These charts provide the investor with a roadmap that clearly depicts the battle between supply and demand. It allowed the outsider to become an insider.

Everyone is familiar with using maps to plan road trips. If we don't pay attention to your navigational devices, you will unintentionally end up in the wrong place. To prepare for a journey with your family, familiarize yourself with the map, check the air in your car's tires, begin with a full tank of gas, and ensure the children have some books and toys. Plan your trip. Most investors never plan their investment trip. The Point and Figure method of analyzing supply and demand and Relative Strength can provide that plan. Nothing guarantees success, but you increase the probability of success significantly when you stack all the odds in your favor.

Somewhere along the road, you may encounter a situation that forces you to detour, but that's okay if you remain committed to your original plan. This book outlines the best plan for financial success when you are investing in securities.

When all is said and done, if more buyers exist in a particular security than there are sellers willing to sell, the price will rise. It doesn't matter the reason people are buying; it just is, and it shows up in the price action. If the number of sellers in a specific security exceeds the number of buyers, the price will decrease. Maybe someone needs the funds for a new house or wants to pay for their daughter's wedding. It doesn't matter why people are selling; it just is. If buying and selling are equal, the price will remain the same. This is the irrefutable law of supply and demand. The same reasons that cause price fluctuations in produce, such as potatoes, apples, and asparagus, cause price fluctuations in securities.

This book is designed to teach you how to formulate your own operating system using the Point and Figure method coupled with Relative Strength.

Although the investment industry is overloaded with different methodologies to evaluate security price movement, I have only found the Point and Figure method and Relative Strength to be straightforward and easy to understand.

The charts are made up of X's and O's. Recording the movement of a security using this method is very much like recording a tennis match. A tennis match can last 12 sets. Each player can win a certain number of sets, but the final count determines which player wins the match. In the Point and Figure method, we are only interested in the culmination of the match, not the winner of the underlying sets.

The patterns this method produces are simple and easy to recognize-so simple that I have taught this method to grade 6s in Allen, Texas near Dallas. I have always maintained that simply is one of the best.

Frances E Norton Elementary School Allen Texas – Grade 6 Gifted class

My sister Karen is an Elementary teacher at Frances E Norton in Allen, Texas. She is the Gifted and Talent Specialist at her school. One day, she called and asked if I could teach her grade 6 class about the Stock market. In our first Skyped encounter, after introducing myself, I asked them if any of them owned a business. They looked at me as if I was from Mars. I then asked if any of them had jobs. Again, they stared at me with bewilderment. So I told them that the first thing we had to do was to get in groups of 3 and start a business. "*A make-believe business?"* they asked?" "NO; an actual business that either made something or offered some type of service"; and off to work they began.

I wanted them to experience firsthand failure, to pick themselves up and start again. That is what we face with investing. Not everything works the way we hope it will. Some parents complained and didn't want their children involved. When those children found out that their parents didn't want them to go through the exercise, they were livid. Everyone participated. The groups came up with some pretty amazing products and services. With more children like these, I know that our future will be in good hands. I wanted them to keep the profits, but my sister had them give the profits to a local charity.

The next step was to talk about growth from an individual proprietor to a partnership to a limited company to a listing on the exchange how the company raises capital, and so on. Every so often, Karen would call me and speak in a hushed tone, and I would ask her where she was calling from. *"....From the closet, they've asked a question I don't know the answer!"*

The next part of the program was to teach them how to chart. We selected a local company, Texas Instruments, and charted it using Point & Figure. Over the course of a month, they were all marked on their charting abilities.

The last step was to teach them security selection as they had entered a regional stock-picking competition for Central Texas. I provided them with data on the S&P 100 and the NASDAQ 100. You could tell that some teams had their parents help them. They selected names like Walmart, Johnson & Johnson, and so on. They are good companies but lousy stocks. Only one group had truly grasped what I had taught them and went on to win the competition, beating out a middle school that had won it 7 years in a row.

And the best part was each kid won $50.

The concept underlying any method of analysis you choose must be valid. Supply and demand are as valid and basic as it gets. I do not question the validity of other methods. Why not make it a part of your everyday investing? Why complicate it? I don't think that the extra analysis in an attempt to gain an edge really works out.

It builds in rigidity when you need to be flexible. Keep the rules simple but follow, more importantly, follow them.

I chose Point and Figure and relative strength because it helps remove the emotions when selecting and viewing a stock. Without a doubt, emotions are the greatest cause of bad decisions in the stock market and life. How many times have you looked at a stock to buy only to be told it has poor fundamentals? You change your mind and decide to pass on it, only to watch it soar. On the opposite side of the equation, are you thinking of selling a stock only to hear that the talking heads on TV are predicting its continued climb, only to watch it reverse and tank?

These are just some emotions we constantly confront as investors. You have to have a plan and a road map to deal with the bumps along the way. Point and Figure and Relative Strength may not always be right, but they will be over time.

Many investors ignore the construction of PnF charts because we have software that does it for us now. However, knowing how to construct the chart is vital to understanding because it will help explain the behavioral and psychological reasons behind the moves.

The Point-and-figure method of analyzing stock movement simply records this battle between supply and demand in a logical and organized way, as it was designed. The word organized is the key. A basic road atlas would be difficult to use if the actual lines depicting the roads and interstates were missing. It is the same in the stock market business. Looking at an endless list of High-Low-Close quotations on any stock can be equally confusing. Besides, you would go blind. However, organizing these quotations logically makes the battle between supply and demand much more evident.

The point-and-figure chart simply shows whether supply or demand is winning the battle. It doesn't show volume, merely the price, because that is what we are interested in. It doesn't matter what an analyst or the company says. All that matters is the price. All this information shows up in the price. Remember, we are only interested in the battle between supply and demand.

From a historical perspective, we credit Charles Dow with creating it. The Point-and-Figure didn't come into existence through creation or invention but rather out of necessity. In 1900, one needed to record price movements on the fly while standing on the exchange floor or in front of the ticker tape. One's notes might look something like this. [37]

9¾ 10¼ 11½ 11¼ 12½ 12¼ 13¼ 15 16½ 15 14¼ 13½ 12
10¼ 10 11¾ 11½ 14 15 16 17 19½ 20 21¾ 19 18¾ 19½ 20

US markets traded in fractions until 9 April 2001. We all learned and traded with fractions those days. Back to the story: Dow quickly realized he should drop the fractions and just record the full number. His record might look something like this.

9 10 11 11 12 12 13 15 16 15 14 13 12 10 10 11 11 14 15 16 17 19 20 21
19 18 19 20 21 19 18 19 20 20 21 23 20 19 16 15 13 12 10 10 8 9
11 11 14 15 16 17 15 11 12 12 13 12 12 13 15 16 15 13 12 10 10 11 11
14 15 16 17 19 20 21 19 20 20 23 24 21 22 22 20 19 19 20 22
20 21 20 21 20 19 19 20 19 20 20 21 22 21 20 20 21 21 22 21
20 19 19 18 19 19 20 19 20 19 19 18 18 17 18 17 16

Looking at this array, it is difficult to find the high and the low of the day or where most of the

[37] Du Plessis, J, 2006, *The Definitive Guide to Point and Figure,* Harriman House, Hampshire, Great Britain, pg28

trading took place. All you can see is the opening at 9 and the closing at 16.[38]

You can start to see that boxes are being formed, which has led to other developments. We start to see changes in the notations, with X's representing when a security is rising and O's for when it is declining.

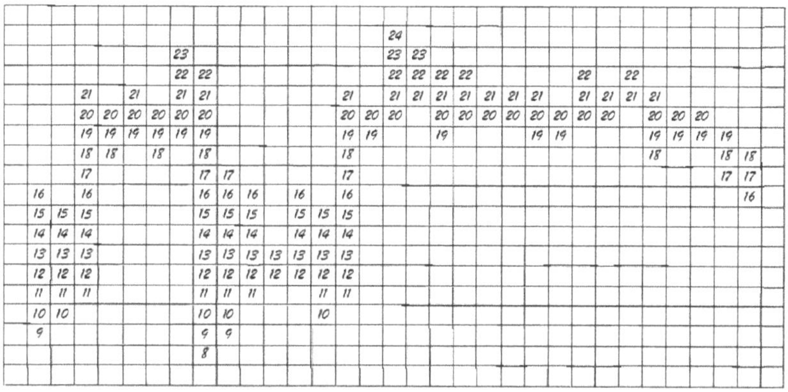

Figure 1-4: Early record of prices

A.W. Cohen[39] is credited with the creation of the 3-box reversal method seen below. In this example, each box represents $10. You can see that the PnF 10x3 chart is much cleaner.

[38] Du Plessis, pg32

[39] Cohen, A.W., *How to Use The Three-Box Reversal Method of Point & Figure*, Chartcraft., 9th edn,1968, Larchmont, N.Y.

Day no.	Price	Plot Box	X/O	Day no.	Price	Plot Box	X/O
1	1100	1100	X	26	1122		
2	1105			27	1133	1130	X
3	1110	1110	X	28	1125		
4	1112			29	1139		
5	1118			30	1105		
6	1120	1120	X	31	1132		
7	1136	1130	X	32	1122		
8	1121			33	1131		
9	1129			34	1127		
10	1120			35	1138		
11	1139			36	1111		
12	1121			37	1122		
13	1129			38	1111		
14	1138			39	1128		
15	1113			40	1115		
16	1139			41	1117		
17	1123			42	1120		
18	1128			43	1119		
19	1136			44	1132		
20	1111			45	1133		
21	1095	1100	O	46	1147	1140	X
22	1102			47	1131		
23	1108			48	1159	1150	X
24	1092			49	1136		
25	1129			50	1127		

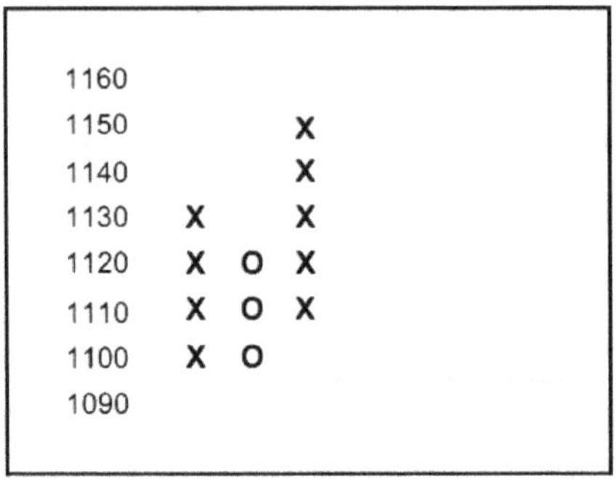

PnF charts have a number of advantages over traditional line charts.

1. They filter out the noise associated with insignificant price moves.

2. They focus on the importance of price movements.

3. They also remove the factor of time in the analysis process.

4. They provide automatic and subjective trend lines.

5. They make the identification of support and resistance lines much easier.

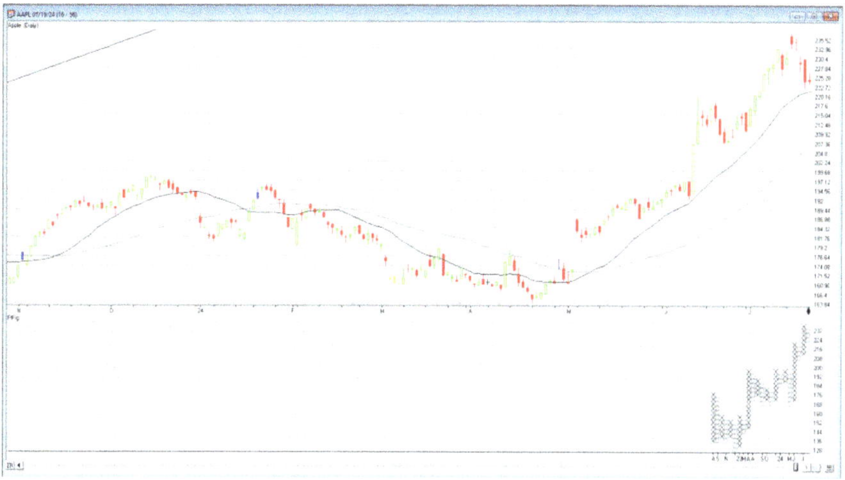

This is a line chart of Apple and below is the same data in Point & Figure. The PnF cuts out the noise and the sideways action of the line chart.

14. Putting it all together

Computer Hardware and Support

While I've stressed the importance of principles, planning, focus, and emotional balance, the absence of the right computer and support system can be a costly oversight. It's a crucial puzzle piece that can't be ignored.

In the current digital era, technology is not just a tool, but a necessity in the stock market. The emergence of online and algorithmic trading platforms has made reliable computer hardware a non-negotiable for traders. As technology continues to advance, the stock market's reliance on sophisticated computer hardware and technical support is only going to increase.

I have always prioritized computer equipment and support. Honestly, the computer sale at Best Buy won't cut it. Slow or outdated computers can cause missed opportunities. High-speed internet connections, powerful processors, and adequate storage are all necessary components for efficient trading. The stock market is a complex and unpredictable environment that requires quick decision-making and precise execution.

Technical support is not just a luxury but a necessity for traders dealing with the complexities of modern computers. Whether it's troubleshooting hardware issues or resolving software glitches, reliable technical support can significantly enhance a trader's performance and peace of mind. Stress reduction is key. Dependable technical support can offer swift assistance, preventing costly downtime and ensuring seamless trade execution.

From my experience, the impact of reliable computer hardware and technical support is undeniable. Traders who invest in these resources and have access to knowledgeable support staff are better equipped to seize market opportunities and manage risks. It's one less thing to worry about. By optimizing their hardware setup and leveraging technical expertise, traders can gain a competitive edge in the market. Good computer hardware and technical support can enhance trading efficiency, improve decision-making, and increase profitability.

For the past fourteen years, I have gotten all my equipment and support from EZ Trading Computers (https://eztradingcomputers.net/) because Eddie Z is a veteran trader who trades every day and knows our environment. He and his staff understand that the essential qualities of a successful Trading Computer are speed, reliability, after-the-sale support, and multiple monitor support. I agree with him that the most important reason traders need a Trading Computer is to avoid "slippage."

Slippage occurs when using a lower-end computer that does not display price information in real-time. Although the price data may be off by just a fraction of a second, it's enough to throw off your entire trading methodology.

Have you ever seen a panel discussion on CNBC where the participants are working remotely? Have you ever noticed that sometimes, when the interviewer asks a question, there can be a long delay before the panelist answers? Or do the panelists wind up talking over each other?

This happens because each panelist has a different computer and a different internet speed. This oversized "pause" is a delay. Slippage is a very similar phenomenon, and it costs traders a bundle.

Most traders don't realize that mass-manufactured computers and the mainstream processors from just a few years ago just can't keep up with today's mega levels of streaming price data.

I have all my systems custom-made by Eddy's team. It is like getting a custom-tailored suit rather than picking something off the rack. As for the support, I have never experienced this level before in customer service. Imagine, if you will, driving your Formula 1 racing car and coming into the pit for a tire change. In seconds, they perform a tire change, and you are back on the track. I have had times when I reported an issue to my support team, and before I am back at my desk from getting a coffee, they are already dealing with the problem.

Looking ahead, the future of computer hardware and technical support in the stock market will likely be shaped by advancements in artificial intelligence, machine learning, and automation. These technologies have the potential to revolutionize trading strategies, optimize hardware performance, and enhance technical support services. Traders who embrace these innovations and adapt to the changing landscape of the stock market will be well-positioned for success in the years to come. Be ahead of the curve.

For the outsider looking at what I do, it may appear to be just random action. It may appear to have no pattern for buying and selling. Why are these specific securities chosen instead of others? Sometimes, security is bought only to be quickly sold out. Sometimes, security is held for years.

I see relative strength as a heat-seeking missile that is always on the hunt for better returns. Constantly assessing what to purchase and what to steer clear of is essential. I am a relentless return zealot who is eliminating or weeding out underperforming assets and replacing them with better performers. I see underperforming assets as a cancer to your account returns, and I want to act as dispassionately as a surgeon's scalpel to remove them. I trained my clients to perceive securities in the red or sell zone as a dangerous tumor that demanded immediate removal. Not tomorrow or next week, but right now.

I love this quote from Senator Everett Dirksen.

"I am a man of fixed and unbending principles, the first of which is to be flexible."

This statement perfectly captures the truly paradoxical truth of relative strength investing — flexibility and discipline. Can you imagine the grief I would have been in IF I had not taken the sell signal on the GTAT trade? It surprised me immensely after they went bankrupt. I went back to check the signals to see if, by chance, there was something else that had prompted me to sell it out. Was it divine intervention or just my discipline kicking in? It was truly humbling because it could have been just as easy to let it slide.

In the financial markets, the term flexibility conjures up images of black box algorithms and whimsical decisions, with seemingly different rationales for every transaction. This is further from the truth.

I consistently build models that have a great deal of flexibility, yet the rationale for every trade is the same—relative strength rank. I liquidate a current holding due to a significant decline in its relative strength rank, and I purchase a new position with a favorable relative strength rank. I buy strong positions and hold them for as long as they remain strong.

Any virtue, taken to an extreme, can become a vice. Flexibility is good if it results in better investment results than a static allocation. However, if flexibility is taken to an extreme, it can lead to overtrading and poor investment results. Likewise, discipline is good, but it can become a vice if it results in an inability to adapt to different market environments.

I have tinkered and played around with various model configurations, such as having the rankings signal trigger on shorter time frames. I have found these attempts as not pleasing or successful. In the portfolios I build, I make great efforts to find a healthy way to have both flexibility and discipline.

I have mentioned this once before, but it is worth repeating. My strategy and selection process is simple yet very robust and, more importantly, adaptive. I start with a selected universe of securities. I then rank each one against the other on a price-performance basis until I have a list of the strongest performers ranked to the weakest. This process not only gives me the strongest to consider but also the weakest to avoid. A disciplined implementation strategy of adapting to trends as they change can provide robust returns without pinpointing tops and bottoms. It has proven to be an effective approach, and I use it. You don't need to hold for the entire swing up or down; you just want the fat middle of the move. Remember, you are buying from someone who is thinking it is time to sell.

This reminds me of a discussion I had once with a manager. This manager liked to start each of his meetings with a few minutes of chit-chat before getting to the actual purpose of the meeting. In this one particular meeting, he started asking me what the price of gold was. He had been busy all morning and could not check on the markets. I informed him of its stability and upward drift. He then asked about the price of oil. I told him again where it had been trading that morning and the levels of some of the energy names. I opened up a little and let my guard down a little to say that I felt it could go lower, and I had a price target of XXX. I can't remember that actual price.

Well, he responded in a loud, matter-of-fact, condescending tone, "It won't." Maybe he knew something I didn't. I didn't know. I timidly said that is what my charts are telling me right now. It could be mistaken, but that is what they are saying. He then opened up a little to say that he had been a buyer six months earlier in December, but he wasn't looking that smart right now, as they were all down. All I said was a muted, "Oh, in December?" He then asked why I said that. I paused momentarily and said "Because that is when I was selling. Thank you for buying my stocks." The rest of the meeting did not go well.

Hobo Investing

Investing, at its core, is a simple process. During the 1930s depression, one way for the unemployed to move from one area to another was to jump aboard a freight train moving in the direction they wanted to go.

In a sense, our investing stance is similar. We are mobile, not tied down to any specific place or position. We don't have to hold things we don't want to. The direction in which the market is moving is where we can and will go.

The first thing we need to do is determine if the train is going north or south or just sitting on a track siding doing nothing. Once you've found a train going north, you only need to hop aboard. If the train starts to go south, you need to jump off, remembering Jess Livermore's rule about cutting losses short.

The concept is simple, but sometimes investors make the execution more complicated. For us, relative strength and trend following provide the tools and methodology to find the northbound trains. The same tools and methodology can be used to tell you when the switch engine has come along and started to move the train south.

The problems happen when investors deviate from the simple goal-directed hobo mentality and get too clever for their own good. Can you imagine how irrational some investors' behavior must look to a hobo?

Here are the top six dysfunctional hobo sayings:

1. I wanted to go north, so I hopped on an out-of-favor southbound train, hoping it would go north, eventually. (value investing hobo)

2. I got on a northbound train, but it only went north a few miles. A switch engine came along and started to take my boxcar south. How embarrassing! This train owes me. I'm not getting off. (ego-attached hobo)

3. There are so many trains going north. I want to hop on one eventually, but I'm afraid it will go south right after I get on it. (failure to launch hobo)

4. This northbound train is picking up speed. I'd better get off. (premature ejection hobo)

5. I wanted to go north, but my train pulled onto a siding and stopped. Maybe I'll just sit here and see what happens. (buy-and-hold hobo)

6. There are so many trains going north without me. Eventually, they will all have to go south, and then I'll have my revenge! (bitter hobo with an economics background)

If you want to go north, get on a northbound train. KISS really applies here. Keep it simple, Silly. On our good days, we all know this, but it's so easy to forget.

Graph 5 - Point and Figure chart of Priceline (PCLN) October 20, 2017.

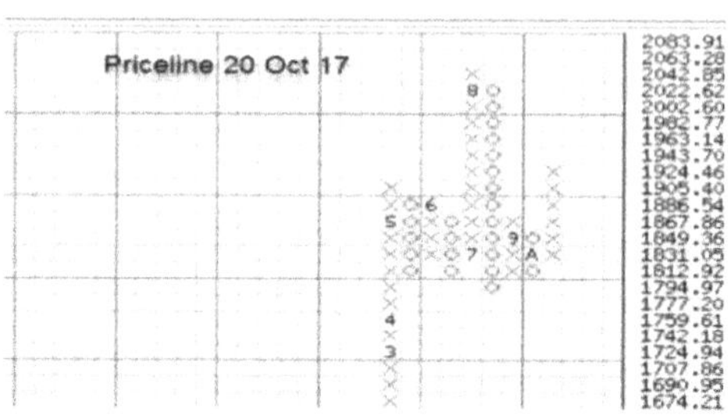

On the evening of Friday, October 20, 2017, I ranked the S&P 100. I noticed Priceline had fallen from the Don't Buy More zone into the Sell Threshold.

The Method says that if a stock falls from the Buy or Don't Buy More Zone past the Sell Threshold (position 25), sell it and, with the proceeds, buy the highest-ranked stock you don't already own. Simple. Don't overthink it, just do it.

If we look at the individual stock itself, it doesn't look too bad. It had been on a sharp rise since January of 2017 and had run into resistance in May-June. It bounced around for the summer, making a run to new highs in August, but slammed into selling pressure. At the beginning of October, it looked like it was going to challenge the high in August. Still, relatively, other stocks were performing better, and it pushed Priceline lower in our rankings, so it had to go, and something else came in. No emotions, just act.

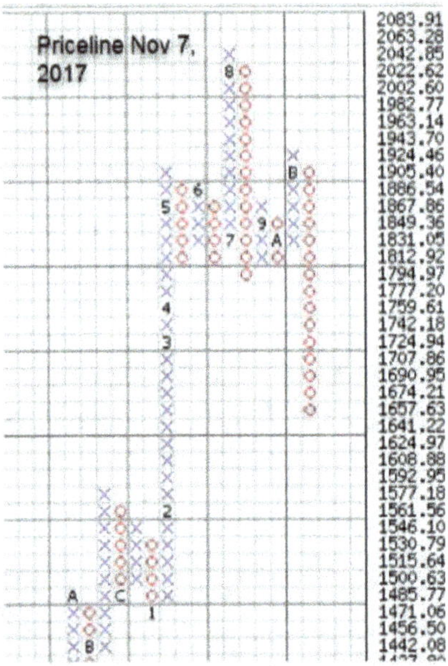

So I called the client holding it and told him what had happened. I suggested selling it on Monday at the open and using the proceeds to buy PayPal, which we did. On Monday morning, the stock opened at $1950.00. I entered my trade a few minutes later and got a fill at $1954.825.

On November 6, they reported earnings below consensus estimates and lowered their forward guidance. The next day, it dropped like a stone to a low of $1,638.10 and closed at $1,645.72. A drop of over $309 or -15.5% from where we sold it. Did I have inside information? No. Did I read something that predicted this? No. I can say that I sold it because my rules told me to sell it, and that is what I did. Does it work every time? No. It works overtime.

Why isn't everyone using this strategy?

That is a valid question. I've pondered over it myself many times. Several reasons hinder the widespread adoption of this strategy. Many times, when we receive a signal to either buy or sell, there may not be a clear, interesting, fundamental reason to do so. You simply can't find a fundamental basis for action. With GTAT, I faced open ridicule for selling. The manager didn't appreciate my comment about him buying my energy stocks when I was selling, especially since they had fallen since my sale. But I stood by my decision, even in the face of criticism.

At first, purchasing at a high cost proved to be quite difficult. It feels unnatural. We are hardwired to seek out a bargain to obtain things at a lower price. However, Constellation Software is a perfect example of my learning experience. I will tell you that you will get used to it. In the end, you won't care about the initial discomfort. Yes, you will miss out on the cocktail party stories of the great exploits of the great bargains you picked up. Leave those for others.

It seems unnatural to let the winners ride. Most advisors will tell you to cut or trim the winners and buy more of the losers. Average the cost down. Here is a picture of the famous hedge fund manager, Paul Tudor Jones, who made billions in the market. He employed trend-following strategies such as relative strength and other technical analyses. He was a firm believer in taking small losses and had a major focus on risk control. It is also very hard for many people to take small losses. Everyone likes to be right. When you are selling at a loss, you are wrong. The ego kicks in and won't let you forget it.

Remember, early on, I mentioned that in the portfolio used in the Beyond ETFs Pro app, there had been 245 winning trades and 248 losing trades. There have been more losers than winners, yet the return generated from 2 January 2007 to 30 June 2024 has been 20.21% annualized. The average hold period for the winning trades was 175.64 days, while the loser's average hold period was 63.96 days. The S&P 100 index is 8.03%.

Holding the course becomes especially difficult during market turning points. We don't pick the exact bottom or exact top. I have never seen a system that picks the exact top or bottom. It is a trending following methodology, and we are willing to give up some at the top and wait to get in at the bottom. We are interested in only the meat in the middle of the move.

What I like about relative strength is that it is adaptive and changes as the markets change. It requires discipline and commitment.

Here is an example of The Brockmann Method at work with a portfolio using the Toronto Stock Exchange 60, the 60 largest stocks in Canada. Blackberry was the darling of the International markets back then. It entered the portfolio and gave us a sell signal, never to be bought again. Today, the stock does not exist.

BlackBerry: within the S&P/TSX 60 Model

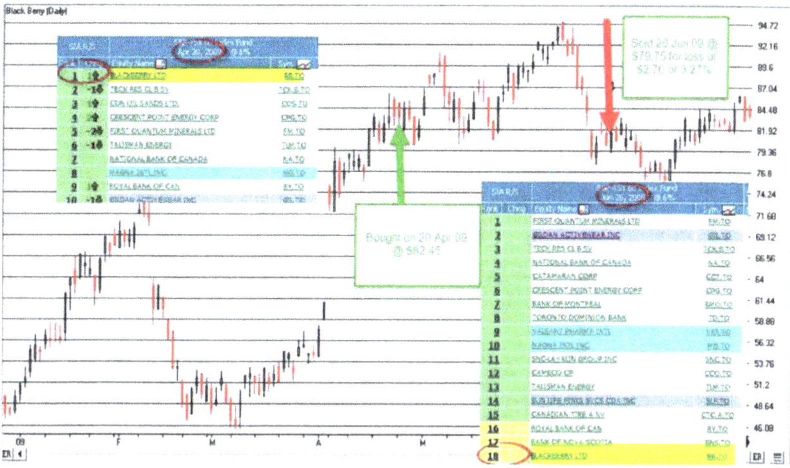

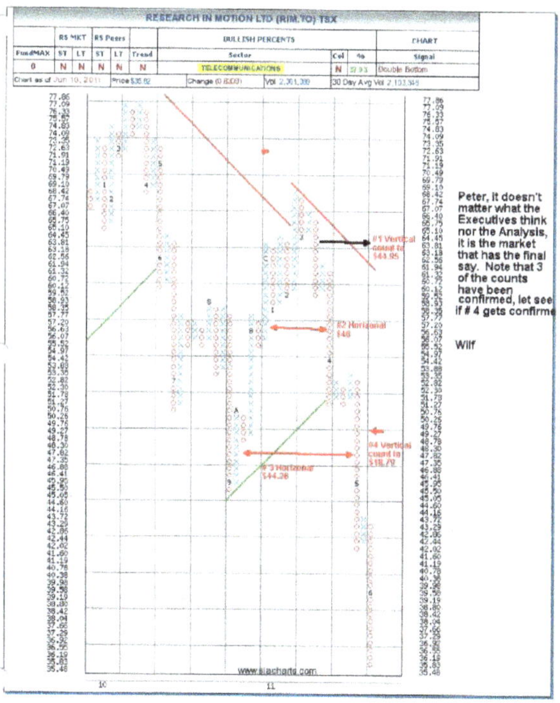

Peter asked me if Blackberry was a buy. I said NO.

15. The Birth Of Beyond ETFs Pro

Peter's Challenge

From the website: https://beyondeftspro.com

{Peter Brockmann} "*You're probably in the same place I was in March 2017. I stared at my name-brand, so-called 'professional' advisor's quarterly report. It was about half of the performance of the S&P 100 index. I was disappointed, I was mad, and I was depressed. To top it all off, my wife reminded me we still paid them 1% for that poor performance!*

Time for new thinking. "You're so FIRED!"

{Wilf Brockmann} I remember the call from Peter in which he proudly announced to me that he had FIRED his broker. He had taken action, and you could tell by the sound in his voice. He told me how his advisor had consistently underperformed the general market indexes. That he had basically been invested in everything under the sun. After he had finished, I asked him, ...so what are you going to do now?" There was a long pause, and then he says, "I guess I'll buy the index; at least that way, I will beat my old advisor and not pay those high fees." I says, "Wouldn't you rather BEAT the index? You deserve better." I tells him I was coming to Boston and would explain the entire process to him, and the rest is history.

{Peter Brockmann} That's why I built this app with his financial analysis know-how. Wilf is the CEO of Brockmann Analytics and Trading, who created the Brockmann Method. Beyond ETFs Pro brings his 45 years of investment knowledge together with the discipline of an AI machine designed software system to share market insights and let you know the score.

Truly, it became history. Peter had been dealing with a financial advisor at a major investment Bank for years until the broker retired. The new broker in the interview used all the buzzwords you would expect. The company recommended asset allocation, the efficient frontier, our analyst recommends, our fee-based platform, and so on. You get the picture. To be honest, it seemed like someone had taken a shotgun and blasted at the markets to ensure every aspect of Peter's 401(k) account was covered.

It had ETFs representing large cap, small cap, growth style, value style, blended style and bonds. The theme or focus of the account was 70% invested in equity ETFs and 30% bond ETFs. I suspect his new advisor was relatively new to the business and transformed the account into a hodge-podge of every ETF under the sun. I would call it the "you can't sue me" type of portfolio. Remember what Warren Buffett said, 'You concentrate to gather wealth; you diversify when you don't know what you are doing." I would say nothing else about the advisor, but I would say that Peter sold everything out and moved the account so he could manage it himself.

So I said to him, 'What are you going to do now?" because he sounded really pleased with himself for taking his first step in financial independence. "....Errr, I'm not sure. I haven't thought that far. Maybe I will just by the index," he said. I said to him: "Why settle for just beating your broker, why not beat the index as well? You desire better," He said, "You can do that? "I thought that most active managers don't beat the index". Again, he told me he could put his money into a market index ETF and still beat his advisor. When I told him he deserved to beat the index, he responded I had told him in the past that most professional money manager don't beat their respective indexes. It's true, but with my process, he and you would too.

These charts are from SPIVA, a S&P Dow Jones Indices data division as of December 31, 2023.[40] You may ask why professional money managers cannot beat their respective benchmarks. There have been claims whispered about job security being one reason. Yes, it's pretty cynical, but if a manager is in the middle of the pack in terms of performance, they would be less likely to get axed than an outliner at the bottom of the heap. The same would be true of advisors. Being average is less stressful than being an outlier. The client's profitability decreases, but the manager and advisor remain employed. We are not in the business of keeping them employed but for you, the client, to prosper. Your prosperity is our ultimate goal and the driving force behind our work.

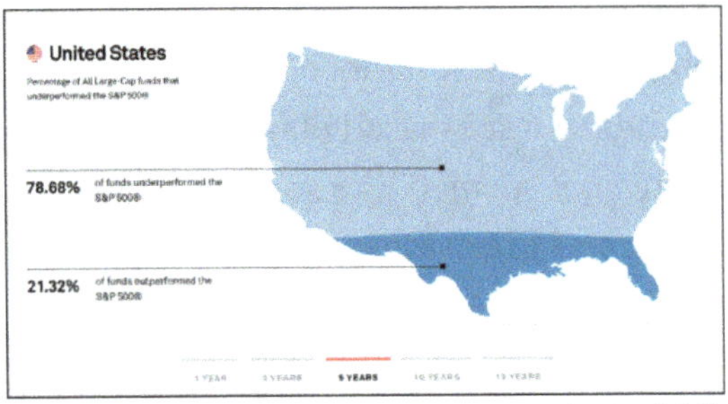

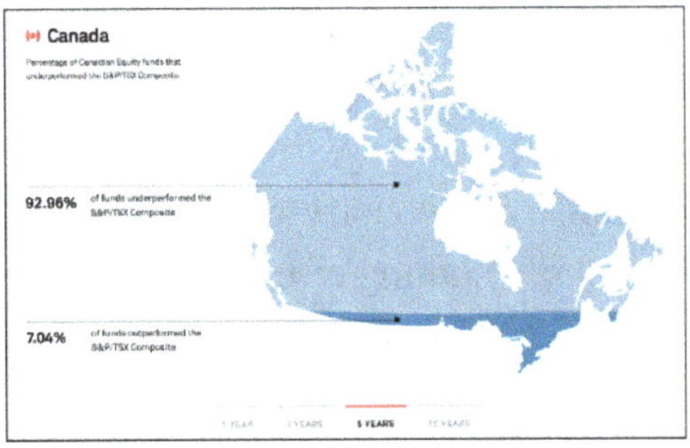

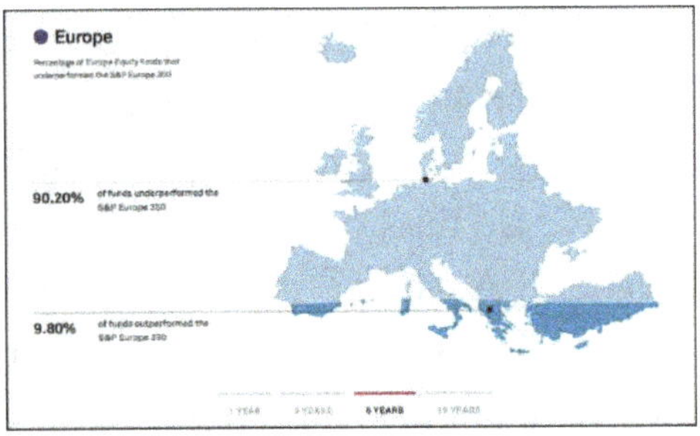

One would expect active managers to thrive in a stock picker's market. Theoretically, these managers should do what we do: pick the winners and avoid the losers. This potential for success keeps the market dynamic and exciting.

[40] https://www.spglobal.com/spdji/en/research-insights/spiva/?utm_source=pdf_spiva#us

However, managers face regulatory oversight in the amount of weighting each position can be within the portfolio. Also, the mandate stipulated in the prospectus could restrict the manager. For example, it might only allow the manager to hold a specific percentage within an industry group or for individual securities. So, technology might blow the doors off in performance, but the manager might only be allowed a certain amount.

Jason Zweig[41], in his article in the Wall Street Journal on 5 July 2024, pointed out that the three largest stocks in the S&P 500 (Microsoft, Apple, and Nvidia) made up nearly 21% of the total value. The five biggest stocks represent 27%, and the top ten account for 36%. At this time, active managed funds held on average only 14.2% of the top three stocks and 20.8% of the top five, well below the concentration of the index.

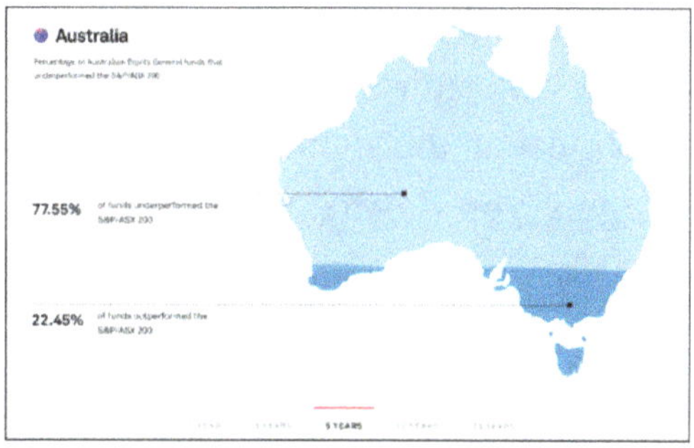

These figures hold true with most other regions as well.

To be honest, pick any time period in which active managers underperform their respective benchmarks. Concentration might be the excuse this year, but not for other years.

By the way, in case I haven't shared this with you before, I've experienced the consequences of underperformance firsthand. Because of performance-related issues, some clients have ended our relationship. It is a fact of life, and it keeps me all humble. This

[41] Zweig, J., *'Why Your Fund Manager Can't Beat Today's Stock Market'* Wall Street Journal, 5 July 2024

transparency is a testament to our commitment to learning and improving in the financial industry. Relative Strength works over time, not every time. In times of sideways or violent markets, it does not perform well.

Boston Bound

I traveled to Boston and sat with him and his wife, Anne. The explanation I gave them was that when you purchase an ETF Index, you are actually buying all the stocks that are part of that index. I asked them if the energy or material sectors were underperforming. It drags the entire basket down. What if the Technology sector is shooting out the lights, and you still have the healthcare sector dragging you down? You don't get the upward performance you deserve.

I told them I use the S&P 100 universe because it contains the 101 largest companies in America. It holds household names like Apple, Amazon, Nvidia, Exxon Mobil, and Bank of America, to name a few. To put the S&P 100 size in perspective, it represents about 54% of the entire US equity markets as of 2020.

I explained that I rely on relative strength because of its adaptive nature and long-term track record of success. Relative strength is simple in concept yet powerful in application. Relative strength is simply comparing price performance within a universe of securities. Here, the stocks make up the S&P 100 index. Analyzing securities by their relative strength provides a way to identify the leaders from the rest of the pack. Our goal is to own those market leaders. Relative strength also allows us to identify the laggards. Successful investing also requires avoiding big losers.

We rank the entire index daily from top to bottom and compare each stock to every other in the index using a price comparison. Price is the final arbitrator. It doesn't matter what the analyst or the company says. All that matters is the price and relationship it has with others. Witnessing the action of supply and demand. I told him that studies have shown us that securities that have been performing well for the last 6 to 12 months continue to perform well for the next 6 to 12 months. Similarly, those who have performed poorly over the same time frame will continue to perform poorly as well.

What I have found is that this is often more accurate than experts. Relative strength is a handy way to measure price and gauge market participants' actions. There's no guarantee that they will do the same thing tomorrow, but perceptions change gradually over time as new information comes to light or new thinking about old information emerges. Staying with strong relative strength trends and departing when they weaken is the simplest way to stay in synch with the changing flow of information in the market.

Peter is an iOS engineer. He develops and tests apps for a living. Once he heard and understood the power of this process, we had to share it with the world.

Welcome to Beyond ETFs Pro.

The future of investing has arrived. With our innovative AI investing approach, you will unlock the secrets of the stock market. By harnessing the power of price momentum, our algorithm ranks the top 100 companies in America every evening, guiding you on when to sell and what to buy. Leave your emotions behind and let our machine AI make objective decisions for you. Join us and discover a new era of profitable investing.

Two remarkable aspects of this app and its core investing system exist.

One is that it works and works really well. The Brockmann Method, rigorously applied, has been shown to generate a return of more than six times greater than the S&P 100 since 2007.

An initial investment of $100,000 on 2 January 2007 in each of Beyond ETFs Pro Model and S&P 100 index would be worth $2,510,844.62 as of 30 June 2024, not including dividends in Beyond and $406,607.61 in S&P 100.[42] Please remember that past performance is no indication of future performance. Our approach works over time, but not every time.

The second aspect is that it is so simple. Beyond ETFs is designed to exploit simple economic principles combined with many academic researchers' insights. It is a rules-based, proven, and elegant methodology to beat the Index. Beyond ETFs, it leverages AI machine computing power so you can assess your score in real time.

Buying the right stock is only half of the success equation. Telling you when to sell is the other.

We do that with Beyond ETFs Pro.

[42] Records found with Brockmann Analytics and Trading.

/beyondetfspro.com

BAT

Annualized returns of

Beyond ETFs and S&P 100

*	S&P100	Beyond	# of Trades** total	winners	losers
2007	3.84	43.29	34	19	15
2008	(-37.06)	(-6.04)	10	8	2
2009	19.13	43.88	22	16	6
2010	10.07	29.13	37	28	9
2011	0.87	(-1.92)	30	18	12
2012	13.38	25.83	32	19	13
2013	27.4	48.83	33	26	7
2014	10.27	17.79	35	23	12
2015	0.34	6.98	35	19	16
2016	8.78	(-5.58)	58	19	39
2017	19.34	26.34	31	20	11
2018	(-5.8)	(-4.65)	39	15	24
2019	29.57	19.27	59	39	20
2020	19.3	25.45	46	21	25
2021	27.64	18.2	44	32	12
2022	(-22.22)	(-5.77)	44	14	30
2023	30.84	56.52	36	23	13
2 Jan 24 to 30-Jun-24 ***	18.29%	45.31	25	18	7
02-Jan-07 to 30-Jun-24 Annualized	8.25%	20.21%	493	245	248
Average days held			119.46	175.64	63.96

* Figures are annualized rates
** Open trades are included in these figures
*** Returns to the date stated.

Note that at the bottom of the chart is the length of holdings. The average hold of a winner was 175.64 days, and of losers, 63.96 days. We really do cut short the losers and let the winner ride.

We generate an average of 30-40 trades per year.

16. Extended Reach

I have a five-foot rule. If you come within five feet of me, I will smile and say hello. I'm sorry, I just will. It doesn't matter who you are; everyone gets the same treatment. It doesn't cost me anything to do that. Something else I do is if you ask me how I am doing, I respond with, '*I'm Perfect."* We all know the question of how you are is a simple way of being polite. It's the same as, 'Nice weather, hey. Most people are caught off guard by the perfect comment. It shocks them, it's not expected. My next response is, "If I were any better, I'd be your twin." So they think I'm nuts. So be it.

One Sunday, I attended a Spanish-speaking church service. They had a social gathering afterwards, which I attended because they offered coffee and treats. Many of the people and families in attendance were new immigrants from South America seeking a new life. I am so fortunate to be born here and have not had to endure the many hardships they might have had to have gone through. They chose to leave their neighbors, family, and the life they were accustomed to. I selected a table for which I did not know anyone and asked to join them. Nice people and we talked, and I got to practice my Spanish along with enjoying the coffee and the treats. I must have handed my business card to someone because I received the following email a short time later.

Equities

From Carlos XXXXXXX on 2023-10-14 6:11 pm

Dear Mr. Wilfred P,

I hope this letter finds you well. My name is Carlos XXXXXX, and I am pleased to reach out to you regarding the business card you provided to my wife, Ines, who attends St. Francis-Martin. We have learned about your distinguished career as a professional trader, and we are intrigued by the possibility of benefiting from your expertise and guidance.

Over the past eight years, I have been involved in the world of trading, exploring various aspects, from the foreign exchange market (Forex) to US stocks, options, and cryptocurrencies. My focus has been on technical analysis, complemented by a solid understanding of fundamental analysis. Despite my years of experience, I have experienced ups and downs, with more losses than gains. Nevertheless, my passion for trading remains undiminished, and I am determined to improve and grow in this exciting field.

I understand that trading is an art that requires time, patience, and an experienced mentor to guide me along the way. This is why I dare to write to you today, seeking your guidance and support. Your experience and knowledge in Brockman Analytics and Trading Equities Options Futures would be invaluable to my development as a trader. If you are willing to consider the possibility of becoming my mentor, I would be more than grateful.

I thank you in advance for your time and consideration. I eagerly look forward to the opportunity to learn from your experience and continue growing in this fascinating world of trading. Please do not hesitate to contact me at any time through this email or by phone at [XXX-XXX-XXXX] to discuss any further details.

I thank you again for your attention and look forward to your response.

Sincerely, Carlos XXXXXXX

Re: Nice to meet you Carlos

From Carlos XXXXXXXX on 2023-10-21 1:08 pm

Details Plain text

Dear Wilf,

It was a pleasure meeting you, and I genuinely appreciate your insights and wisdom on trading. I'm eager to learn and grow here in Canada, and I believe your guidance will be invaluable.

Thank you for sharing the results of the positions in the S&P 100 universe. Your approach of letting the market determine a stock's value rather than personal bias is a valuable perspective. I completely agree that following a system, even when it involves buying at highs and accepting losses, is a crucial part of successful trading.

Your case in point with TSLA is a great example of the importance of sticking to a system. It's a testament to the discipline required in trading, even if it can be tough.

I'm preparing a list of questions, and I'll certainly reach out once I have them ready. Your willingness to help and share your experience means a lot to me.

Once again, thank you for your time and valuable insights.

Regards,

Carlos

El sáb, 21 oct 2023 a las 12:29, <wilf@brockmann.com> escribió:

Nice to meet you, Carlos,

I hope anything I said or mentioned today will help you grow here in Canada. The more successful you become, the better we all are.

I placed the two positions into the S&P 100 universe with the following results.

ABNB - rank #57 LMND - rank #101 out of 103

As I mentioned, I let the market tell me the value it places on a stock. It doesn't matter what I think; it is the market that has the final say.

A couple of reasons why people have difficulty grabbing hold of this system are that people always like a sale, we always want a deal and we want to buy stuff cheaper. Buying at a high is a little nerve-racking for most people. The second reason is that people hate taking losses. Most of the time, they will hold on until they break even. One has to be like a robot and follow the system.

Case in point. Back on July 7, 23, we bought TSLA into the model at $274.43. On 15 Aug 23, we sold it on a sell signal at $232.84 for a loss of -14.42%. Ouch. Yesterday, it closed at $211.99, down another -9%. Double ouch.

When you make a list of questions to ask, let me know.

Regards,

Wilf

Brockmann Method

From CarlosXXXXXXXXX on 2023-10-21 11:34 pm

XXXXXXXXX

Dear Mr. Wilf Brockmann,

It is a pleasure to greet you and, express my admiration for your remarkable personal story and career in the world of investments. Your journey from childhood insurance to the creation of the "Brockmann Method" is truly inspiring.

I have taken an interest in your investment approach and am eager to learn more about your strategy and investment philosophy. As someone who is eager to delve into the world of trading and investment, I have compiled some specific questions that I would like to pose to you. I understand that your time is valuable, and I would greatly appreciate it if you could provide me with your guidance.

- What is your approach to risk management in your strategy? How do you handle potential losses?

- What is the typical duration of an investment in your strategy? Do you have a short or long-term focus?

- How do you determine the size of your positions in different stocks in your portfolio?

- Do you have any specific advice for maintaining discipline and following your strategy even in times of volatility or uncertainty?

- Do you use leverage in your strategy? If so, what is the leverage-to-capital ratio you consider appropriate?

- If an investor has limited initial capital, such as $3,000, how would you recommend starting to implement your strategy? Is there a minimum account size you suggest?

- What percentage of your account are you willing to risk on a single trade? How do you determine this percentage?

- How do you manage the size of positions in your portfolio? Do you use an equal-weight approach for all positions, or do you vary the size based on certain criteria?

- In case of a series of losses, do you have rules or limits for temporarily reducing the size of your positions or taking a break from trading?

I am confident that your answers will be invaluable for my development as a trader and investor. I thank you in advance for your time and consideration.

Once again, congratulations on your achievements and dedication to the world of investments. I look forward to the opportunity to learn from your experience.

Sincerely, Carlos

Great questions

To Carlos XXXXXXX on 2023-10-22 1:47 pm

Carlos, keep the questions coming. Here are some short answers for the time being. I will fill in the gaps with more details later.

1. What is your approach to risk management in your strategy?

Response: Risk management is embedded within the implementation of the strategy itself in three ways. Firstly, in Beyond ETFs Pro, we select the top ten positions. This gives us diversification by not putting all our eggs in one basket. In theory, we should place everything in the number one position. However, reality and emotions dictate a more prudent course of action. I have found that the optimum number for Beyond ETFs Pro is ten. I have other portfolios in which the optimum number is six. Why not 15 or twenty positions, you ask? Remember what Warren Buffett said, "You concentrate to garner growth; you diversify if you don't know what you are doing."

The second point is that the more names you add to the portfolio, the weaker each new name is, thus weakening the entire portfolio. We are focusing on the strongest. More names do not make it safer. In fact, I have found that it increases the turn rate as the lower-ranked positions are sold, and new ones are bought more frequently. This is besides the slippage that occurs with the constant buying and selling, commissions paid, the difference between the bid and ask price, and so on.

The third point is that the system will trigger a sell recommendation as a position underperforms its peers. Remember I told you about the GTAT story? People following relative strength would have left Enron and Nortel well before their final collapse and, with Enron before the financial fraud was uncovered. In Enron's case, all we knew and could see that there were sellers of the stock, and the pressure continued, forcing it down the ranking score. The system is adaptive, and by following it, we are always in the sectors and stocks performing better relative to their peers. I have seen Ford ranked dead last to rise to the number one position. Why? I don't know. But just like in the TV series Dragnet, Sgt. Joe Friday's line is so appropriate. "Just the facts, ma'am, just the facts." We let supply and demand told us what the market is thinking. That is all we care about.

Question #2. How do you handle potential losses?

Response: Let me re-phase this question: How do you handle the EMOTION of potential losses? I hate to break it to you, but we will have losses. Get used to it. Sorry, but that is the reality of investing and trading in the markets. It is called "risk-taking". Otherwise, it would be called 'sure-thing taking."

I will not enter a trade unless it has a greater potential of being a winner than a loser. I want the probability of success on my side. I will not flip a coin and hope for the best. By the way, praying is an excellent strategy for saving your soul but not your trading account. So don't let a position get to the state when you feel you have to pray about it.

The beauty of the Brockmann Method is that it will tell when to get out of a position. The position will have lost its ranking and has declined, and something else is ranking better. I want to be with better. There is a saying that goes like this: your last breath is essential but not as essential as your next breath. The same is true with investing. Your last trade was essential but not as important as your next trade.

I will come back to the emotional mindset of investing and trading later.

Question #3. What is the typical duration of an investment in your strategy?

The duration of a trade depends on the market and the activity we are encountering. We can go what would seem like months without a trade, and then suddenly, it seems like something needs to be sold every other day and something else bought. The markets will sometimes require a rotation out of certain stocks and sectors into others. Sometimes, it is a violent and quick shift. Other times, a more gradual rolling over.

You can see that we want to hold the winners and sell the losers.

Account Statistics/Analysis **Beyond ETFs Pro**

		Winners	Losers
Start date:	01/02/07		
End date:	10/20/23		
Number of trades:	477	234	243
Average periods per trade:	117.92	174.83	63.12
Maximum Profit/Loss:		165.36 %	(39.88)%
Average Drawdown:	(5.96)%	(3.44)%	(8.39)%
Average Profit/Loss:	6.52 %	19.88 %	(6.34)%
Probability:		49.06 %	50.94 %
Average Annual ROI:	20.18 %	41.50 %	(36.67)%
Reward/Risk Ratio:	3.02		
Portfolio:			
Starting Balance:	100000.00		
Ending Balance:	1506597.09		
Gain/Loss:	1406597.09		
Gain/Loss (IRR) %:	1406.60 %	Annualized:	17.51 %
Drawdown:		From	To
Maximum Continuous:	(15.16)%	06/07/22	06/17/22
Portfolio High:	(6.13)%	07/19/23	07/24/23
Peak/Valley:	(30.47)%	02/19/20	03/23/20

The average winner was held from 2 January 2007 to 20 Oct 2023, 174.83 days. The average loser was held only for 63.12 days.

Question #4. Do you have a short or long-term focus?

The focus of the Brockmann Method and Beyond ETFs Pro is longer-term in nature. Over the years, I have tinkered and played with settings and calibrations to attempt to create the optimum parameters. To date, it uses end-of-day data for its calculations. Factors in play include price slippage, commissions, differences between bid/ask spreads and others.

In time, I do not doubt that with the help of AI and faster and more powerful computing power, the algorithm will be adapted to incorporate all the moving parts.

Brockmann Method

From Carlos XXXXXXX on 2023-10-22 2:49 pm

Dear Mr. Wilf Brockmann,

I hope this message finds you well. I greatly appreciated your previous response and am excited to learn more about your investment approach. However, as I delved deeper into researching your method, a concern arose that I would like to share with you.

I have been truly impressed by your extraordinary track record of performance. Nevertheless, my concern revolves around how to adapt your method to smaller trading accounts. If I had a capital of $500,000, I would not hesitate to invest in your system, as it has proven to be a capable option for generating a substantial annual income, supported by a robust risk control – something I highly value. But in my case, I have a smaller account, approximately $3,000. It is evident that generating consistent profits with an account of this size to eventually reach a more significant capital, such as $500,000, may pose additional challenges. As my goal is to become a successful investor and trader, I would greatly appreciate it if you could provide advice or specific adaptations that you believe would be beneficial for investors with more modest accounts.

Furthermore, given your unquestionable success and expertise, I would like to point out that your strategies could be particularly beneficial if you ever consider expanding them to Latin America. In this region, trading accounts are usually of smaller size compared to other developed markets. Countries like Mexico, Colombia, and Brazil, for instance, present growing financial markets with substantial potential. Your strategies, tailored for more modest accounts, could offer significant opportunities for Latin American investors.

Once again, I thank you for your time and consideration. I am eager for the opportunity to learn from you and look forward to your guidance on this matter.

Sincerely, Carlos

Hello Carlos,

The only way I know how to quickly turn $3,000 into $500,000 is to rob a bank or win the lottery, or maybe going to the casino and placing all on red. I wish there was any other way.

The law of probabilities is the same for a large account as for a small one. That is the reality we live in. You mentioned that you had some experiences with losses in the market. I suspect the risk level was slightly higher than you had expected. I didn't ask because we all have been there.

We thought out a plan and it did not work out. We all have done that.

One of the first things I said when we met was that people need to have two accounts. One was their investment account, and the other was their trading account. The trading account comes after one has an anchor with their investments. Believe me when I say I have blown up my trading account every which way to Sunday. I have made and lost many a fortune.

The only difference between $3,000 and $300,000 is the number of zeros and the mindset. If you succeed with a strategy employing $3,000, you will be set for life. I have tinkered with different parameters, different instruments, and different markets and have yet to find a continuous successful get-rich-quick program.

I attend several presentations every week to listen to people and their approaches. I could tell you about the options program I created in which my trades generated returns of 5-10% a week on invested risk capital, BUT the music changed, and so did that portion of my trading account.

There are plenty of people willing to sell you a dream. Sorry, I don't have a rapid account accumulation program. The Brockmann Method sometimes does have spurts of massive growth, but I don't know when.

Keep the questions coming. I will also keep answering your list of questions.

Regards

Wilf

I followed up with Carlos with an article from Bloomberg about Venezuela's leading opposition candidate.

Re: I thought you might find this interesting

From Carlos XXXXX on 2023-10-27 11:33 pm

Good evening Wilfred,

I hope this message finds you well. I want to express my apologies for not responding to your previous message in a timely manner. Life has been quite hectic lately because of my commitments in the dental assistant program. I've been grappling with a lack of motivation and a sense of sadness. While I long to immerse myself in the world of financial markets, my studies and recent financial responsibilities have left me with very little time to do so. My mind is constantly preoccupied with market movements and global dynamics, but my body is stuck in classrooms and working long hours as an Uber driver to maintain financial stability. I understand that this is a temporary phase and all part of the process, but there are moments when bitterness creeps in.

On a more positive note, I want to extend my heartfelt gratitude for sharing information about Venezuela with me. Maria Corina Machado seems like a remarkable potential presidential candidate, and I would wholeheartedly support her. Unfortunately, in my home country, the central government's control over public powers has led to a distorted electoral process. The three rectors responsible for overseeing elections are closely aligned with the current president, Maduro. This has resulted in a consistent pattern of rigged elections, leading to a significant exodus of Venezuelan migrants seeking better prospects in other countries. The people feel detached, and those who dare to protest in the streets often face imprisonment or worse. In Venezuela, the very idea of freedom remains more theoretical than tangible. The recent disqualification of Maria Corina from holding public office has rendered the primary elections she won a symbol of the uphill battle for change.

Wilfred, I look forward to hearing from you soon and having the opportunity to sit down for a coffee. Until then, please accept my warmest regards and best wishes for a pleasant weekend.

Sincerely,

Carlos

El mié, 25 oct 2023 a las 10:35, <wilf@brockmann.com> escribió:

17. One more thing – OK, a few more things

Shiny new objects

People have long shown a tendency to desire the newest, shiniest object that is just out of our reach, as observed by researchers. This inclination extends beyond material possessions and we can also see it in the world of investing. In making investment decisions, individuals often abandon strategies proven to work in favor of those perceived as offering more promising returns.

This behavior stems from various factors, such as fear of missing out on potential gains, cognitive biases, and the influence of marketing and media. Plenty of historical events bear this out, but why is this behavior played out, and what is the impact of this tendency to chase after the latest investment fad?

The Tulip Mania of the 17th century in the Netherlands and the dot-com bubble of the late 1990s are not just historical events, but cautionary tales that resonate in the current investment landscape. These episodes, marked by speculative frenzy and subsequent market crashes, highlight the dangers of investing based on hype and speculation rather than sound fundamentals.

In more recent times, the dot-com bubble of the late 1990s has served as another cautionary tale. During this period, investors poured money into internet companies with little regard for profitability or sustainability, driven by the belief that the new technology would revolutionize the economy. When the bubble burst in the early 2000s, many investors suffered significant losses as overvalued companies collapsed.

Investors can see the impact of this tendency to chase after shiny new objects in investing through the volatility of financial markets and the prevalence of market bubbles and busts. While innovation and technological advancements have the potential to create significant wealth, they also carry inherent risks that can lead to devastating losses for investors who are not careful.

Influential individuals such as Elon Musk, Jeff Bezos, and other tech titans have captured the investing public's imagination, driving their companies' valuations to astronomical levels. While these visionary leaders have achieved great success, some analysts are sounding the alarm about a potential tech bubble, suggesting that traditional metrics may overestimate the valuations of their companies. Is the meme stock crazy? It's just another sign of this phenomenon.

From a psychological standpoint, cognitive biases such as recency bias, confirmation bias, and herd mentality contribute to the allure of the shiny new object. These biases can cloud judgment and lead to irrational investment decisions. Recognizing and overcoming these biases is crucial for investors to think independently and make informed investment choices.

It is clear that human nature plays a significant role in driving investment decisions. The allure of the shiny new object can be powerful, but investors must exercise caution and discipline to avoid falling into traps that can lead to financial ruin. By examining historical trends, key figures, and psychological factors, we can better understand why investors often abandon what is working for what they are told or think is working better. It is crucial for investors to conduct thorough research, diversify their portfolios, and remain vigilant to navigate the complex and ever-changing world of investing successfully.

If you have a systematic approach that is working, why change? As the saying goes, there are many ways to skin a cat and there are many ways to make money in the markets. You don't need them all. You just need one or two. I know from personal experience. Focus and become a master of your craft.

Conclusion:

This is the Brockmann Method.

An approach to price momentum investing that provides simple signals on when to sell and what to buy. Investors can develop a habit of success by leveraging both knowledge and discipline, which gives them the confidence to make informed investment decisions. It certainly works for our clients. You can put it to work for yourself.

You can find the Brockmann Method in bedded in an app called "beyond etfs pro." Found in both Android and Apple stores. Also at https://beyondetfspro.com.

Check it out. Invest in your success.

Warm Regards,

Wilf Brockmann

www.ingramcontent.com/pod-product-compliance
Lightning Source LLC
LaVergne TN
LVHW052301200926
848481LV00002B/432